The Universal Declaration of Human Rights was adopted by the United Nations General Assembly in 1948. In 1966 the General Assembly adopted the two detailed Covenants which complete The International Bill of Human Rights; and in 1976, after the Covenants had been ratified by a sufficient number of individual nations, the Bill took on the force of international law.

★

At present, few people even know that there *is* an "international bill of human rights." The purpose of this edition is to change that. This is *the* basic document of our times, the strongest, most stirring, most complete description ever of the rights of individuals and the duties of nations. Every citizen of the world should be familiar with this bill, should be able to quote from it, should know what it contains. These rights are too valuable to be entrusted to policy-makers; their only effective enforcement will come through public awareness. Toward this end, we offer The International Bill in book form for the first time.

THE INTERNATIONAL BILL OF
HUMAN RIGHTS

Foreword by
JIMMY CARTER
Former President of the United States

Afterword by
ADOLFO PÉREZ ESQUIVEL
1980 Winner of the Nobel Peace Prize; Coordinator General of the Service for Peace and Justice in Latin America

Introduction by
TOM J. FARER
Distinguished Professor of Law, Rutgers-Camden School of Law; President of the Inter-American Commission on Human Rights of the Organization of American States

Historical Introduction by
PETER MEYER

Edited by
PAUL WILLIAMS

ENTWHISTLE BOOKS
Glen Ellen

Library of Congress Cataloging in Publication Data
Main entry under title:
The International bill of human rights.

  Contents: Universal Declaration of Human Rights—
International Covenant on Economic, Social, and
Cultural Rights—International Covenant on Civil and
Political Rights.

  1. Civil rights (International law) I. Williams,
Paul, 1948–   II. United Nations. General Assembly.
Universal Declaration of Human Rights. 1981.
III. International Covenant on Economic, Social, and
Cultural Rights. 1981. IV. International Covenant on
Civil and Political Rights. 1981.
K3238.A1I533   341.4'81   81-7804
                                     AACR2

ISBN 0-934558-06-X
ISBN 0-934558-07-8 (pbk.)

Type set by Richard Ellington. Design by Ellington and Williams.
Printed in the U.S.A. by Kingsport Press, Kingsport, Tennessee.

First printing.   10 9 8 7 6 5 4 3 2 1

Additional copies ($9.95 cloth, $3.25 paper, plus $1.00
postage per order; write for information on volume discounts) are available from:

ENTWHISTLE BOOKS
Box 611
Glen Ellen, CA 95442 USA

85-3554 WAR

dedicated to Eleanor Roosevelt,
a great woman
with a great vision

CONTENTS

FOREWORD

by Jimmy Carter

During the first year of my Presidency I had the honor of signing, on behalf of the United States of America, the two international covenants on human rights which, together with the Universal Declaration, make up the International Bill of Human Rights.

Both the United States and the United Nations had their origins in a vision of the greatness of the human possibility. The American Declaration of Independence speaks of the idea that, ". . . all men are created equal . . . endowed by their Creator with certain unalienable rights . . . Life, Liberty, and the Pursuit of Happiness . . ." The Charter of the United Nations speaks of ". . . faith in fundamental human rights, in the dignity and worth of the human person, in the equal rights of men and women and of nations large and small . . ."

Though separated by a century and a half in time, these visions are identical in spirit. The covenants that I signed in 1977 are unusual in the world of international politics and diplomacy. They say absolutely nothing about powerful governments or military alliances or the privileges and immunities of statesmen and high officials. Instead, they are concerned about the rights of individual human beings and the duties of governments to the people they are created to serve.

The International Covenant on Civil and Political Rights concerns what governments must *not* do *to* their people, and the International Covenant on Economic, Social and Cultural Rights concerns what governments *must* do *for* their people.

By ratifying the covenant on civil and political rights, a government pledges, as a matter of law, to refrain from subjecting its own people to arbitrary imprisonment or to cruel or degrading treatment. It recognizes the right of every person to freedom of thought, freedom of conscience, freedom of religion, freedom of opinion, freedom of expression, freedom of association, the right of peaceful assembly, and the right to emigrate from one's country.

A government entering this covenant states explicitly that there are sharp limits on its own powers over the lives of its people. But as Thomas Jefferson once wrote about the Bill of Rights which became part of our own American Republic, "These are fetters against doing evil which no honest government should decline."

By ratifying the other covenant on economic, social, and cultural rights a government commits itself to its best efforts to secure for its citizens the basic standards of material existence, social justice, and cultural opportunity. This covenant recognizes that governments are the instruments and the servants of their people.

It would be idle to pretend that these two covenants themselves reflect the world as it is. But to those who believe that instruments of this kind are futile, I would suggest that there are powerful lessons to be learned in the history of my own country.

Our Declaration of Independence and the Bill of Rights expressed a lofty standard of liberty and equality. But in practice these rights were enjoyed only by a very small segment of our people.

In the years and decades that followed, those who struggled for universal suffrage, those who struggled for the abolition of slavery, those who struggled for women's rights, those who struggled for racial equality—in spite of discouragement and personal danger—drew their inspiration from these two great documents, the Declaration of Independence and the Bill of Rights, and from our own Constitution. Because the beliefs expressed in these documents were at the heart of what we Americans most valued about ourselves, they created a momentum toward the realization of the hopes that they offered.

Some of these hopes were 200 years in being realized. But ultimately, because the basis was there in the documents signed at the origin of our country, people's discouragements and disappointments were overcome and these dreams prevailed.

My hope and my belief is that the international covenants and the Universal Declaration that make up this International Bill of Human Rights can play a similar role in the advancement of and the ultimate realization of human rights for individual men and women throughout all nations of the world.

INTRODUCTION

by Tom J. Farer

At his first news conference, Alexander M. Haig—United States Secretary of State under President Ronald Reagan—achieved the unenviable distinction of communicating at a uniquely early point in his tenure contempt for the values which knit up the Western Alliance. The medium for this unintended message was the following statement:

> International terrorism will take the place of human rights in our concern because it is the ultimate of abuse of human rights. And it's time that it be addressed with better clarity and greater effectiveness by Western nations and the United States as well.

In the coderoom of international diplomacy, a declared priority for terrorism over human rights is effortlessly deciphered as an invitation to put on the brass knuckles and never mind the Marquis of Queensberry. Whatever Secretary Haig's actual intentions (and I am not reluctant to attribute to him the best of motives), his language was an incitement to governments to apply forbidden methods for the liquidation of present or potential rebels.

The historical setting of Secretary Haig's remarks makes this conclusion inescapable. Before the Second World War, scholars and diplomats assumed that international law allowed each equal sovereign an equal right to be monstrous to his subjects. Summary execution, torture, conviction without due process (or any process, for that matter) were legally significant events only if the victim of such official eccentricities were the citizen of another state. In that case, international law treated him as the bearer not of personal rights but of rights belonging to his government, and ultimately to the state for which it temporarily spoke. (In effect, the individual was nothing more than a symbol and a capital asset. Assaults on his person carried out or acquiesced in by representatives of another state were deemed assaults on the dignity and material interests of his state, requiring compensation.)

Guardians of the moral realm were episodically less permissive. Virtually from the start of that bloody enterprise known as the Spanish Empire in the New World, Catholic priests struggled to restrain the awful cupidity and cruder fantasies of the Conquistadors, their secular associates in Spain's civilizing mission. In addition, both Catholic and Protestant missionaries worked to alert decent opinion in Europe to the genocidal trade in African slaves and, thereafter, to such abominations as Belgian King Leopold's personal empire in the Congo.

Even Leopold's fellow monarchs had no stomach for his methods of organizing labor, which included the mutilation of sluggards and drop-outs. And so, while completing the orderly division of Africa at the Congress of Berlin in 1885 and the Congress of Brussels four years later, they announced and Leopold nominally accepted certain standards to be followed in treating the indigenous inhabitants. Since the Conference provided no enforcement machinery, relying rather on the ineffable Leopold, that noble gentleman carried on business as usual. Nevertheless, the very recognition of limits on Leopold's caprice was a rare early instance of formal concern for and legal restraint on a sovereign's discretion in the disposition of his human assets.

Pogroms in Russia, the massacre of Armenians in Turkey and Maronites in Lebanon, as well as the efforts of governments to wrap raison d'état in a higher morality (as in the Anglo-French effort during the First World War to portray the conflict as a struggle between good and evil, and the half-hearted attempt after the War to prosecute the Kaiser as a war criminal), all helped erode the long-entrenched perception that what went on within a state was not a matter of legitimate international concern unless it affected the material interests of aliens. But it was not until the final stage of the Second World War that governments first took the leap from moralizing rhetoric to legal action.

They were driven by popular revulsion over Dachau and the other charnel houses operated by the Nazis, by a surge of idealism sharpened through confrontation with Nazi ideology and, perhaps, by the victors' natural desire to equate success and virtue. In succeeding decades, the community of nations, old and new, established a thicket of legal restraints.

For the first time in history, states assumed obligations to their own citizens as precisely and formally defined in many cases as the legal obligations they had hitherto owed to each other under international law (for example, with respect to the immunity of diplomats). Both through formal treaties and informal practice, they bound themselves not to torture or summarily execute their citizens, or to convict them without due process of law or to dissolve their trade unions or to discriminate among them on the basis of race or religion or to do a great number of other things that in earlier ages were matters entirely at the discretion of sovereigns.

The Charter of the United Nations was the point of departure for this unique legal development. The Charter includes among its purposes, "promoting and encouraging respect for human rights." More pointedly, in Articles 55 and 56, dealing with international economic and social cooperation, "All Members pledge themselves to take joint and separate action in cooperation with the Organization for the achievement of . . . universal respect for, and observance of, human rights and fundamental freedoms for all without distinction as to race, sex, language, or religion." In order to translate these generalities into measurable rights and obligations, the United Nations General Assembly adopted without dissenting vote, on

December 10, 1948, the Universal Declaration of Human Rights.

The International Bill of Human Rights consists of the Universal Declaration and two subsequently adopted covenants. Since the United Nations Charter makes most resolutions and declarations of the General Assembly merely recommendatory, the Declaration itself had a somewhat ambiguous legal character. Initially, at least, most governments and legal scholars thought it expressed compelling moral values rather than legally binding norms. To cure doubts about the Declaration's legal force, as well as to refine and elaborate its contents, leaders of the human rights movement urged preparation of what finally became the separate Covenants on economic, social and cultural rights and on political and civil rights.

The Declaration passed through the United Nations quickly and rather easily. The Covenants, on the other hand, had to struggle for years towards a difficult and contentious birth. Divisions of ideology and interest, lightly foreshadowed in the debate over the Declaration, acquired unmistakable prominence once the member states began turning the Declaration into hard law.

It was one thing for governments to endorse the non-binding, unpoliced standards of the Declaration; quite another to contemplate specific legal obligations and machinery to enforce them.

Very few governments exhibited conspicuous enthusiasm for the proposition that the international community should measure their performance against well-defined standards and publicize their failures. While most states shared varying degrees of uneasiness about enforcement machinery, two distinct groups warred ferociously over the demand that freedom from want (that is, economic and social "rights") be treated on a legal *and* moral par with freedom from fear (the right to personal security), freedom of religion and freedom of speech.

The United States and several other capitalist democracies led the opposition against a coalition of Communist and developing states.

In order to accommodate the anxiety over supervision and the war over economic and social rights, the drafting committees finally agreed to produce separate covenants. One would cover economic, social and cultural rights, essentially the values we associate with the welfare states which began to flourish in Europe and North America after World War II. The second would incorporate political and civil rights. A state could adhere to either or both Conventions without coincidentally accepting any very significant enforcement authority. Article 41 of the Civil and Political Covenant, which allowed one state to charge another with non-compliance, was "optional." And machinery permitting individual complaints against states was built into an "optional protocol" which to this day relatively few states have accepted.

The General Assembly approved both Covenants and the Optional Protocol in 1966. It took another ten years to secure the number of ratifications necessary to bring them into force, i.e., to bind those states which had in the interim ratified them.

Failure rapidly to convert the Declaration into binding agreements with enforcement machinery helped sustain the natural cynicism of a world where atrocity is an everyday affair. Diplomats, hardly less than ordinary people, often overlooked the many other human rights agreements which were exerting pressure on governments even before the Covenants became legally enforceable.

At the universal level, various conventions prepared by the International Labor Organization were particularly important. Inspection teams dispatched by the ILO to check compliance with the forced labor conventions produced damning reports which apparently led to improved working conditions in Liberia and Portugal's African territories.

The countries of non-communist Europe and the Western Hemisphere took the essential norms of the Universal Declaration and embodied them in regional conventions (see Appendix II and III for excerpts from these documents). In addition, they established systems of surveillance and enforcement—human rights commissions and courts—which go far beyond the monitoring procedures now available at the United Nations.

For people living in either region, the first line of defense in case of an attack on their rights is formed by the regional commissions, the Inter-American Commission on Human Rights and the European Commission of Human Rights. Both possess broad investigative powers. The Inter-American Commission not only investigates individual cases, it has also inquired into the general situation of human rights in various countries including Argentina, Chile, Cuba, El Salvador, Haiti, Nicaragua, and Uruguay. Its very detailed and comprehensive reports are public documents available at the offices of the Commission in Washington and through information outlets of the Organization of American States.

Cynicism about the International Bill of Human Rights does not spring exclusively from ignorance and the related assumption that human rights function exclusively in a moral rather than legal realm. Cynicism is also fostered by the spurious belief that attention to human rights inhibits the struggle against "terrorism." Of course, the frantic efforts governments make to conceal violations of human rights in campaigns of extermination against rebels and dissidents of all kinds implicitly concede the moral and legal force of the standards being violated. But the beneficial effects of this concession are no doubt offset by the success governments have achieved in convincing otherwise decent people that concern for human rights is an insupportable luxury in an era haunted by terrorism.

Insidious under any circumstances, this form of justification for atrocious behavior threatens human rights on an enormous scale particularly because the term "terrorism" is now employed with a total lack of discrimination. Historically it referred to certain intolerably cruel and viciously indiscriminate methods that even in the midst of civil or international wars were forbidden. These methods have been used by subversive enemies of governments and also by governments attempting to repress opposition.

It is certainly true that in the life of any nation, threats to the public order or to the personal safety of its inhabitants, by persons or groups that use violence, can reach such proportions that even authentically democratic governments may feel compelled to suspend the exercise of certain rights. The International Bill takes account of such emergencies. Article 4 of the Political and Civil Covenant allows participating states:

> In time of public emergency which threatens the life of the nation . . . to take measures derogating from their obligations under the present Covenant to the extent strictly required by the exigencies of the situation . . .

Restrictions may, for example, be imposed on the freedom of information or the right of association. In rare and extreme cases persons may be detained for short periods without specific charges being brought against them. Such measures inevitably endanger the rule of law, but this danger can normally be contained by responsible governments: if they register arrests and inform the families of the detainees of the detentions; if they issue strict orders prohibiting torture; if they carefully recruit and train security forces, weeding out sadists and psychopaths; and lastly, if there is an independent judiciary to correct swiftly any abuse of authority.

Certain fundamental rights, however, can never be suspended, among these, the right to life, the right to personal security and integrity, and the right to due process. In other words, under no circumstances may governments employ summary execution, torture, inhumane conditions of detention, or conviction by a process which does not adequately distinguish guilt from innocence.

In this regard, it is useful to recall words spoken by His Holiness Pope John Paul II to the Organization of American States on October 6, 1979. After acknowledging that at times special measures may be adopted, he added the following:

> . . . they never, never justify an attack on the inviolable dignity of the human person and on the authentic rights that protect this dignity. If certain ideologies and certain ways of interpreting the legitimate concern for national security were to result in subjugating man and his rights and dignities to the State, they would to that extent cease to be humane and would be unable, without gross deception, to claim any Christian reference. . . . A kind of security with which people do not identify, because it does not protect them in their very humanity, is only a farce; as it grows more and more rigid, it will show symptoms of growing weakness and rapidly approaching ruin.

Each government that confronts a subversive threat must choose, on the one hand, the path of respect for the rule of law, or on the other hand, the descent into state terrorism. Hence one can see why Secretary Haig's declaration noted above reflects at best a remarkable confusion. For it obscures the fact that violations of basic human rights are the essence of terrorism whether the violations are perpetrated by private entrepreneurs of atrocity or by governments themselves.

Politically-motivated terrorism is carried out in democratic societies with the precise intention of provoking a terrorist response from the security organs of the state. Such a response tends to polarize the society and fuel sympathy for subversives.

A just and self-confident society has the toughness and resilience to fight back within the limits of law and morality. In waging war against a society which honors those limits, the terrorist campaign manages only to consolidate the community and to reenforce community values and morale. The campaign must therefore fail. A society already divided by injustice and riddled with merited guilt will usually respond with counterterrorism and thereby fertilize subversion while sapping the strength and authority it struggles to preserve.

The International Bill of Human Rights is not merely the codification of our highest values. It is as well a formula for the effective defense of democratic societies from the impulse to terrorism among the enemies of freedom and within our own tortured hearts.

THE INTERNATIONAL BILL:
A BRIEF HISTORY

by Peter Meyer

Where, after all, do universal rights begin? In small places, close to home—so close and so small that they cannot be seen on any maps of the world. Yet they are the world of the individual person; the neighborhood he lives in; the school or college he attends; the factory, farm, or office where he works. Such are the places where every man, woman and child seeks equal justice, equal opportunity, equal dignity without discrimination. Unless these rights have meaning there, they have little meaning anywhere. Without concerned citizen action to uphold them close to home, we shall look in vain for progress in the larger world.

—Eleanor Roosevelt[1]

Barely had the fifty government delegations officiously settled themselves down in San Francisco that spring of 1945 than they were reminded of the most important lesson of the Nazi holocaust: human dignity belongs not to sovereign states but to sovereign individuals. Were it not for a few of those individuals at that Charter-writing session of the United Nations, the new international organization would have given human rights and fundamental freedoms, as observer John P. Humphrey has noted, "only a passing reference."[2]

To Humphrey, later appointed the United Nations' first Director of the Division of Human Rights, it was clear that what saved the Charter from this omission were the lobbying efforts at the San Francisco conference by a number of small countries and by the representatives of some forty-two private organizations brought in by the United States as consultants.

The latter group were the "spokesmen in the corridors"[3] on behalf of human rights. They were responsible for making the promotion and encouragement of "respect for human rights and for fundamental freedoms for all without distinction as to race, sex, language or religion"[4] one of the main purposes of the U.N. They were responsible for the mandate given to the General Assembly to initiate studies and make recommendations which would assist in the "realization of human rights and fundamental freedoms without distinction. . . ."[5] They were responsible for the order to the Economic and Social Council to "set up commissions . . . for the promotion of human rights."[6]

The delegates from Chile and Cuba pushed for Charter articles that would specify and guarantee human rights. Panama wanted a separate bill of rights included in the Charter. Though these proposals were rejected as too controversial, they were remembered. And at least the "consultants" had gotten enough momentum and machinery written into the document to open a back door. [See Appendix I, Excerpts from the Charter of the United Nations.]

At the closing session of the conference President Harry Truman opened the door even wider. "We have good reason to expect," he told the delegates, "the framing of an international bill of rights . . . that . . . will be as much a part of international life as our own Bill of Rights is a part of our Constitution."[7] As events would later prove, that was not so much a prophetic statement as it was the beginning of a crusade.

To make good on the promise of raising a standard that would be a passport to justice anywhere in the world would be a difficult and seditious enterprise. For many nations it would require a revolution in the laws, institutions and customs that governed often-lopsided relationships between the individual and the state. For all nations it would mean a radical departure from the hallowed grounds that supported a faith in the sanctity of domestic sovereignty.

However stout the international moral fiber as a result of Hitler's mad havoc, the world was still a house divided: by dozens of shades of political and economic ideologies, by hundreds of thousands of religious, class, cultural and race barriers, by dictators who still enjoyed riding rough-shod over hapless millions. Even as the United Nations was declaring its determination "to reaffirm faith in fun-damental human rights, in the dignity and worth of the human person, in the equal rights of men and women and of nations large and small,"[8] Joseph Stalin was con-tinuing to purge his Soviet state of dissidents, Francisco Franco was consolidating a dictatorship in Spain, Anas-tasio Somoza was grabbing the reigns of power in Nica-ragua, racism was scandalizing the United States.

So to the difficult task of organizing a consensus among world governments was added the gritty compli-cation that a consensus to honor human rights was an agreement to undermine government autonomy. At bot-tom, human rights were an usurpation of state power.

The United Nations wasted little time acting on its human rights mandate. The Economic and Social Coun-cil established a Commission on Human Rights in early 1946 and made its first priority the drafting of an inter-national bill of human rights.

The Commission fielded an impressive list of mem-bers—representatives from eighteen different countries, cutting across the entire political spectrum. It chose as its first "chairman" Eleanor Roosevelt. Its vice-chairman was a Chinese diplomat, Chang Peng-chung, holding a Ph.D. from New York's Columbia University; and its *rapporteur*, a Harvard-educated Lebanese philosopher, Dr. Charles Malik. These three, along with the repre-sentatives from Australia, Chile, France, the United

Kingdom and the Soviet Union, formed the special committee to write the document.

By the time the drafting committee met, just a few months later, the Division of Human Rights in the Secretariat had already prepared a 408-page package of background material that included observations of members of the Commission; draft declarations and proposals submitted by the governments of Chile, Cuba, India, Panama and the United States; relevant excerpts from the constitutions and laws of a majority of the fifty-five member nations; a draft declaration by the American Federation of Labor; and the Secretariat's own outline for a bill of rights. "The eight members of the Drafting Committee," commented the United Nations *Weekly Bulletin* at the time, "have before them perhaps the most exhaustive documentation on the subject of human rights ever assembled."[9]

Even at this early stage, John P. Humphrey's Division of Human Rights had described most of the rights and freedoms that eventually became a part of the International Bill. The Division's draft listed the rights to life, personal liberty, and choice of residence; rights to property, emigration, freedom of conscience and speech and belief and peaceful assembly; rights to democratic elections, education, work and social security. It also detailed rights to protect the individual against government manhandling: freedom from torture, arbitrary arrest and detention, slavery and compulsory labor, arbitrary searches and seizures, oppression and tyranny.

The Division drew such a detailed list, it said, because it wanted the forty-eight-article draft to "cover the whole field of human rights and freedoms." But it said that it was the Commission's responsibility to wrestle with "political considerations" and even assumed that "the views of governments will probably differ on some of the provisions of the draft outline, particularly those relating to the right of property and the freedom of access to professions."[10] (Eventually, the right to property was included in the Universal Declaration but dropped from both of the later Covenants. Access to professions was modified and incorporated in the Declaration and in the Covenant on Economic, Social and Cultural Rights.)

The Division made no comment about the merit or desirability of the articles it outlined. It did, however, feel compelled to make suggestions about the contents of the preamble. These are worth noting because they offer a fairly precise view of the concerns of the Bill's founding fathers and mothers and of the environment in which the Bill was drafted.

First, there should be references made to the United Nations Charter. Here it became obvious that the intensive lobbying by the "consultants" to make human rights an integral part of the Charter paid off. It also became important in the future as arguments arose about the binding nature of the Declaration and the Covenants. The Charter carried a high degree of standing in international law; and tying other international documents to it helped strengthen their own legal standing.

Second, the Division's working paper suggested mentioning a number of different principles which seemed designed to alleviate fears that the Bill would remove the individual completely from the authority of the state and at the same time to make as strong a case as possible for international supervision of human rights. It should be stated that individuals have duties to society; that a person is a citizen of both his state and the world; that there can be no peace unless human rights and freedoms are respected; and, by the same token, that there can be no human freedom or dignity unless war and the threat of war are abolished. Since saving "succeeding generations from the scourge of war"[11] was the organization's first purpose and universally agreed to be an international responsibility, making human rights an *a priori* condition for peace made them also a prime candidate for international concern.

Finally, the preamble should make reference to "the four freedoms." That the *Weekly Bulletin* didn't bother to define the freedoms in its summary of the working paper was testimony to the impact of a single speech made more than six years earlier. Franklin Roosevelt's 1941 State of the Union address was essentially a statement of United States war aims—e.g., a call for the enactment of lend-lease. But it so artfully stood tyranny and aggression against democracy and peace, oppression against freedom, sickness against health and social revolution against economic well-being that it is no wonder that a bill of rights being drafted over the ashes of Auschwitz would make use of it. Not until the final paragraphs did Roosevelt define the "Four Freedoms" that the speech would be remembered for:

> In the future days which we seek to make secure, we look forward to a world founded upon four essential human freedoms.
>
> The first is freedom of speech and expression—everywhere in the world.
>
> The second is freedom of every person to worship God in his own way—everywhere in the world.
>
> The third is freedom from want—which, translated into world terms, means economic understandings which will secure to every nation a healthy peacetime life for its inhabitants—everywhere in the world.
>
> The fourth is freedom from fear, which, translated into world terms, means a world-wide reduction of armaments to such a point and in such a thorough manner that no nation will be in a position to commit an act of physical aggression against any neighbor—anywhere in the world.[12]

Roosevelt set the moral and philosophical tone which would later support the demand for an international bill of human rights. (What many critics of the Economic, Cultural and Social Covenant tend to forget is that it was an American president who first put economic concerns on the world agenda.)

It is perhaps only a small irony that it was Eleanor Roosevelt who was to chair the committee whose task it was to translate her husband's dream into a reality. She set about the work with political finesse, knowing, as her French colleague René Cassin noted, "with remarkable mastery how to employ the philosophers of India and of Lebanon, the American publicists and diplomats, as well as the delegates of ancient Europe and the world of the East."[13]

The skill would be needed. The political hazards of the undertaking were evident from the beginning. At their first meeting in Lake Success, New York, members of the Commission on Human Rights wrestled with priorities whose place have still not been settled. Mrs. Hansa Mehta of India, for instance, insisted that "people must be assured that there will be adequate machinery to enforce the Bill whenever human rights are violated." The Philippines representative stressed the need for a balance between political and economic rights while both Drs. Chung and Malik emphasized the importance that individual rights must have over the rights of nations. "If the proposed Bill," said the Lebanese delegate, "did not stipulate the existence of the individual and his need for protection in his struggle against the State, the Commission would never achieve its intended purpose." Vladislav Ribnikar of Yugoslavia disagreed. He claimed that "the social principle comes first"; that the "new conditions of modern times" make the "common interest . . . more important than the individual interest."[14]

Mrs. Roosevelt attempted to placate all sides by suggesting that the Commission concern itself with four categories of rights: "personal rights (such as freedom of speech, information, religion and rights of property); procedural rights (such as safeguards for persons accused of crime); social rights (such as the right to employment and social security and the right to enjoy minimum standards of economic, social and cultural well-being); and political rights (such as the right to citizenship and the right of citizens to participate in their government)."[15]

By late 1947, in order to reduce the risk that the Bill would be held hostage to ideological differences, the Commission agreed to divide it into three parts: a Declaration, a Covenant, and machinery for implementation. The Declaration would be a statement of principles and as such be more politically palatable than a Covenant which would contain explicit legal obligations. (While Mr. Humphrey has pointed out that the Covenant "would not have been necessary if the Declaration had been meant to be legally binding," he adds that the Declaration's "reception at all levels has been such that, contrary to the expressed intention of its authors, it may have now become part of international law."[16])

As for setting up the machinery to implement the standard, this also was, as René Cassin, the French delegate to the Commission and 1968 recipient of the Nobel Peace Prize, remarked, "infinitely more difficult" than establishing principles. The obstacles arose not just because of the legal implications, said Cassin in 1951, "but because it will effectively internationalize questions that traditionally have been considered domestic affairs of states."[17]

The drafting committee made fairly quick work of the Declaration. It wound its way through the full Commission, the Economic and Social Council (the Commission's supervisory organ) and 81 meetings and 168 proposed amendments of the General Assembly's Third Committee (one of seven special working units of the Assembly) and was put to a vote in late 1948 in almost the same form as that first proposed by the committee.

In the Assembly the Soviet Union found the Declaration defective. Its delegate, maintaining that "the question of national sovereignty is a matter of the greatest importance," claimed that "a number of articles completely ignore the sovereign rights of democratic governments."* He asked the Assembly to postpone consideration of the Declaration until the following year. The Assembly rejected the proposal. And on the night of December 10, 1948, meeting in Paris, the General Assembly adopted the Universal Declaration of Human Rights, 48 to 0. Eight countries abstained from voting: Poland, Byelorussia, Czechoslovakia, the Ukraine, Yugoslavia, South Africa, Saudi Arabia and the Soviet Union.

Despite the dissent, the vote was, as John Humphrey noted, "a remarkable achievement. . . . In less than two years, the organization had been able to agree on the adoption of a text in a matter which was not only rife with difficulties but which went to the very heart of the ideological conflict which had bedeviled the United Nations ever since San Francisco."[19] Never had so many nations agreed to cede so many rights and freedoms to so many people. Eleanor Roosevelt told the Assembly that she hoped the Declaration would be "the Magna Carta of all mankind."[20]

The Declaration was only the first step for the International Bill—a quickstep compared with the eighteen-year march which followed. It was not until 1966 that the two Covenants and the Optional Protocol were

---

*In dismissing the charge that the USSR wanted to subordinate the individual to the state, the Russian delegate provided a good glimpse of the gulf which separated many of the UN members. "In a society where there are no rival classes," he argued, "there can not be any contradiction between the government and the individual since the government is in fact the collective individual. . . . Therefore the problem of the State and the individual, in its historical sense, does not exist. History has already solved that problem in my country. . . . That relationship is expressed in the formula of which all progressive persons are justly proud: 'the Union of Soviet Socialist Republics is the socialist State of workers and peasants.' "[18]

drafted and accepted by the Assembly. The world changed dramatically along the way; a host of new nations crowded into the international forum. More than twice as many nations had a hand in completing the Bill as participated in the drafting of the Declaration, and their impact was reflected in the document that was finally presented to the world in 1966.

The major substantive change was reflected in the new emphasis given to FDR's third freedom, the freedom from want. The first drafters of the Bill had all but ignored the nascent demands for a recognition of economic rights. Of the twenty-five substantive rights defined by the Universal Declaration (Articles 3–27), eighteen recognized the classic civil and political rights (such as freedom from torture, to a fair trial, to vote, of speech and of belief) and only five were concerned with economic rights (e.g., work and an adequate standard of living). The draft Covenant approved by the Commission on Human Rights in December, 1947, but which never reached a vote by the General Assembly, reflected the same emphasis.

By 1951 the picture had changed. The draft Covenant had grown to seventy-three articles but in very rocky ground. At a meeting of the Economic and Social Council its president, Hernán Santa Cruz of Chile, worried that "fundamental differences of opinion . . . have arisen." Some states, he explained, wanted more implementation machinery; others wanted none. Some refused to accept a Covenant with economic obligations—however laudable they were as ideals—because meeting them would depend on the unpredictable nature of the national economy; others argued that those rights could be framed in such a way as to allow for gradual adoption.[21] By the end of the session most of the Council members could agree on only one matter: that "the difficulties which may flow from embodying in one covenant two different kinds of rights and obligations" could not be overcome.[22] The Council's recommendation that two Covenants be drafted was accepted the following year by the General Assembly.

That decision made it possible for work on the Bill to continue. It by no means ended the struggle.

Eleanor Roosevelt's retirement from the Commission in 1953 represented the loss of a moral and mediative force. And her replacement from the United States, according to Cassin, "participated in the work of the Commission . . . with a disinterest injurious to the Covenants."[23]

It did not help that Mrs. Roosevelt's departure, on April 7, 1953, was preceded by a day by a dramatic announcement from the new American administration of Dwight Eisenhower: Secretary of State John Foster Dulles informed the world that the United States would not sign or ratify the covenants.*

Though in different ways—and for different reasons—the Soviet Union was no more helpful. While always a public advocate of the principles of human rights embodied in the Bill, it consistently balked at any international effort to do more than talk about them. "The implementation of the Declaration and the Covenant," ran its often repeated objection, "is a matter which solely concerns the domestic jurisdiction of the States."[25]

In the end it is less remarkable that the Covenants took so long to draft than that they were adopted at all.

---

*This was but one of many signs of America's new isolationist bent during this cold-war period. A year earlier debate had begun on a proposed Constitutional Amendment which would have forbidden the signing of any treaty which "shall authorize or permit any foreign power or any international organization to supervise, control, or adjudicate rights of citizens of the United States. . . ." The defeat of the amendment, which was kicked around from 1952 to 1957, "was due in large measure," according to international legal scholars Louis B. Sohn and Thomas Buergenthal, "to vigorous lobbying by the Eisenhower Administration and its concomitant undertaking . . . not to adhere to human rights treaties."[24]

And what is still more surprising is that in a number of ways they went significantly beyond the parameters of the Universal Declaration.

The right of "peoples" to self-determination, for example, was a radical departure from the conception of the Bill as a standard of individual rights. It was not mentioned in the Declaration, yet turned up as the first Article in both Covenants. The same was true for the provision, in Article 27 of the Covenant on Civil and Political Rights, for the protection of ethnic, religious and linguistic minorities. And as if to emphasize the new role of groups in the rights schema, the drafters felt compelled to add a cautionary Article (47) that "Nothing in the present Covenant shall be interpreted as impairing the inherent right of all peoples to enjoy and utilize fully and freely their natural wealth and resources."

The economic, social and cultural rights Covenant also added a number of new rights while expanding greatly on others. It said that people not only had the right to join trade unions, they also had the right to strike; should be eligible not just for social security but "social insurance"; enjoy not just physical but mental health. While the Declaration said that "motherhood and childhood are entitled to special care and assistance," the Covenant granted maternity leave to pregnant women and required minimum age limits for child laborers. Where the Declaration said that everyone was "entitled to a social and international order in which the rights and freedoms set forth . . . can be fully realized," the Covenant called for "an equitable distribution of world food supplies in relation to need." Where the Declaration spoke to principles, the Covenant got to the nitty-gritty.

Because they were meant to be legally binding documents, the Covenants were especially sensitive to the question of exceptions. How absolute were these many rights?

Each Covenant answered in its own way. The civil and political rights treaty would allow states to abrogate certain rights if a "public emergency" threatened "the life of the nation"; but it cautioned that the actions be limited to what was "strictly required by the exigencies of the situation." And it added that the rights to life, to freedom of thought, conscience and religion, and to freedom from torture and slavery could at no time be abrogated.

That the economic, social and cultural rights Covenant has come to be called "promotional" suggests something of its overall approach. It is more lenient—at least more vague—about derogations. It allows for "limitations as are determined by law." The theme of "progressive implementation" is stressed. For example, it gives states a two year grace period to adopt the "plan of action for the progressive implementation" of free and compulsory primary education. And while the civil and political Covenant states with explicit consistency that "everyone" has a certain right or "no one" should be deprived of a certain freedom, the economic, social and cultural Covenant always compromises with an introductory "the States Parties to the present Covenant" either "recognize the right" or, even less demanding, "undertake to ensure" the right.

Still, the importance of the economic rights Covenant was not in its attitude toward implementation. That the Covenant was even offered a separate place in the Bill of Rights—though an obvious compromise to the "fundamental differences of opinion" mentioned above—represented a major shift in world priorities. It even achieved something of a symbolic victory when, as the two Covenants were presented to the Assembly, it was listed ahead of the civil and political rights Covenant.*

---

*Compared with what has happened in the United Nations since the Covenants were drafted, the victory of the economic rights Covenant represents only a crack in the door. In 1974, for

If the United Nations had set itself the task of drafting a Bill of Rights that would, as its Third Committee once explained, "be acceptable to as many States as possible" yet would not "establish such a low level that all States could ratify them immediately," then its work was a success.[27] There was certainly nothing immediate about the eighteen years of haggling. The standards, especially considering what existed before, are remarkably high. And when the vote was taken, on December 16, 1966, instead of the 48 nations which approved the Universal Declaration, more than 100 world governments said *yes*; none said *no*. The world had its first International Bill of Human Rights. It represented a significant strike against the walls of sovereignty behind which many nations had hidden their pogroms. It was a forceful affirmation of a rather new creed: that human rights were an international responsibility because they belonged equally to each human being.

There was a hitch, however. While governments had drafted these instruments and governments had agreed to them, it was also governments which had made them necessary in the first place. How were these standards, spelled out with such commanding clarity, to be enforced?

Any number of horror stories could keep the question ringing in the world's ear:

• Indonesia withdrew from the United Nations in early 1965 and later that year General Suharto un-

---

example, the General Assembly declared that there was an urgent need for "the establishment of a new international economic order . . . which shall correct inequalities and redress existing injustices, make it possible to eliminate the widening gap between the developed and the developing countries and ensure steadily accelerating economic and social development in peace and justice for present and future generations." And in 1977 the Assembly stressed that "the realization of the new international economic order is an essential element for the effective promotion of human rights and fundamental freedoms. . . ."[26]

leashed a bloodbath of executions which quickly claimed as many as 750,000 lives. The country then asked to be readmitted to the U.N. Its request was granted just in time for Indonesia to register affirmative votes on the two Covenants on human rights.

• Uganda's head of state, Idi Amin, murdering with impunity in the early 1970s, committed some of his worst crimes while serving as chairman of the Organization of African Unity, whose charter promised to "promote international cooperation, with due regard for . . . the Universal Declaration of Human Rights."[28]

• In Guatemala, Chile, El Salvador and Argentina—all of whom cast their votes in favor of the Covenants—torture, murder and terror were to become the principal means of government.

• And no international agreement saved three million people of Cambodia from annihilation at the hands of their government.

The continual railing against anything that smacked of "intervention in domestic affairs" had resulted in a compromise: a document expressing strong standards but offering only weak measures of enforcement. What's more, though unanimously accepted by the General Assembly in 1966, the Covenants were technically binding only on those States which, in a separate procedure, ratified them; and even then, they would not "enter into force" until thirty-five States had officially acceded to them. Article 41 of the Civil and Political Covenant and the Optional Protocol—which set up mechanisms by which States could complain against other States and individuals could complain against their governments—were also applicable only to those States which agreed to be bound by them.

Thus the full story of the Covenants is somewhat different than the General Assembly votes would suggest:

• The Covenant on Economic, Social and Cultural

Rights: in the Assembly 105 nations voted in favor, none against. It did not "enter into force" until January 3, 1976; and as of January, 1981, only 65 States had agreed to be bound by it.

• The Covenant on Civil and Political Rights: in the Assembly 106 nations voted in favor, none against. It only entered into force on March 23, 1976; and as of January, 1981, only 64 States had ratified it.

• Article 41 of the Civil and Political Covenant (complaint procedure among States): It was not until 1979 that it entered into force, after the tenth State had ratified it; and as of January, 1981, only twelve States had agreed to it.

• The Optional Protocol (allowing individuals to make complaints): Even in the General Assembly this met with less than unanimous approval: sixty-six in favor, two against and thirty-eight abstentions. It entered into force after the tenth State had ratified it, in 1976; but by January, 1981, only twenty-five States had accepted it.

But if any of the governments had planned on hiding their ghosts in the clouds of fluffy enforcement measures, they miscalculated. The principles and standards of the International Bill took on a life of their own. The canons of international responsibility for human rights were reinforced time and again after the Universal Declaration.

In subsequent United Nations declarations and conventions protecting refugees, the rights of women, children, and prisoners, and condemning racism, discrimination and genocide, the process of internationalization continued. In almost every case reference was made to the Declaration of Human Rights, strengthening not only that document's moral force but its international legal impact as well. In Teheran in 1968 the UN's International Conference on Human Rights adopted a resolution saying that the Declaration "constitutes an obligation for the members of the international community."[29]

Outside the United Nations references to the Declaration began to appear everywhere. The Preamble to the Peace Treaty with Japan, signed in 1951 by forty-nine countries, obligated the signatories "to strive to realize the objectives of the Universal Declaration of Human Rights. . . ."[30] In the Republic of Rwanda the 1962 Constitution was written with an article that "guaranteed to all citizens" "the fundamental freedoms as defined by the Universal Declaration of Human Rights."[31] "In the period 1948-1973," said the United States Department of Justice, "the constitutions or other important laws of over seventy-five states either expressly referred to or clearly borrowed from the Universal Declaration of Human Rights. In the same period, the Declaration was referred to in at least sixteen cases in domestic courts of various nations."[32]

Regional associations of governments adopted the most comprehensive human rights agreements outside the UN. They either made explicit reference to the Universal Declaration or relied heavily on the work of UN organs drafting the Declaration and the Covenants. Twenty-one American nations meeting in Bogota adopted a Declaration on the Rights and Duties of Man seven months before the UN ratified its Declaration in 1948. At the same time the Congress of Europe expressed its desire for "a Charter of Human Rights guaranteeing liberty of thought, assembly and expression as well as the right to form a political opposition."[33] Less than three years later, seventeen countries ratified in Rome the European Convention on Human Rights. [See Appendix II.]

In 1959, the Foreign Ministers of the governments of the Organization of American States met in Santiago and decided that "the climate in the hemisphere is ready for the conclusion of a Convention—there having been similar progress in the United Nations Organization and in the union known as the Council of Europe in the setting of standards. . . ." The Ministers established an Inter-American Commission on Human Rights and in 1969 twenty OAS members adopted the American Convention on Human Rights.[34] [See Appendix III.]

In January 1981 the Organization of African Unity announced plans to adopt a charter of "human and people's rights" and establish a special commission empowered to investigate allegations of human rights violations.[35]

A new twist in the thread of international human rights agreements occurred when work began in 1972 on the Conference on Security and Co-operation in Europe. It was neither a strict regional affair nor a treaty-making enterprise. The result, however, was a massive document, some 40,000 words long, that was signed in 1975 by thirty-three European states (every country in Europe, including the socialist bloc, except Albania), and by the United States and Canada. While most of the Helsinki Final Act deals with measures to enhance detente, economic cooperation and military security, a ruckus was quickly made over its human rights provisions. The thirty-five nations agreed to abide by the standards of the International Bill and in what was called Basket III—the Act's section on "Co-operation in Humanitarian and Other Fields"—they spoke in detail about guaranteeing a freer flow of people, information, culture and science across the East-West divide. [See Appendix IV.]

Such an effusion of international declarations, covenants and treaties, regional conventions, provisions in domestic constitutions and court decisions all either referring to or borrowing from the Universal Declaration was unprecedented: in the number of documents agreed to and the singleness of purpose which seemed to push the whole process on. By this gradual but persistent accretion the human rights standards of the Universal Declaration were woven ever more tightly into the fabric of international law.*

If there is any consolation to be gotten from the recent massive violations of international law, it is that at least there is now an international law to be violated. "How much worse would it have been if there were *no* standards?" asks Roberta Cohen, a Deputy Assistant Secretary of State for Human Rights in the Carter Administration. "At least we now know that there are such things as human rights."[37]

"We see hope in the development of standards," says Gerhard Elston, the Executive Director of Amnesty International/USA. "These documents are good if only because they set a measure by which governments can be judged. They may not obey the rules, but at least now we can say to them, 'You have violated standards that you and all governments have jointly set.' No government is immune to public pressure."[38]

The pressure has been a constant companion of the principle-setting process since the initial spade-work on the U.N. Charter by the outside "consultants" in 1945. The first meeting of the Commission on Human Rights, in January of 1947, was attended by representatives from the International Labor Organization, the American Federation of Labor, the International Co-operative Alliance and the World Federation of Trade Unions. To the second meeting came the International Federation of Christian Trade Unions, the World Jewish Congress, the International Federation of Business and Professional Women, the American Federation of Labor and a dozen

---

*In a remarkable application of this law a United States Federal Appeals Court in 1980 allowed two Paraguayan nationals to sue a Paraguayan policemen, then in the U.S., for allegedly torturing a member of their family to death in Paraguay. In an amicus curiae brief the U.S. Justice Department had argued that it was consistent with both international and domestic law for U.S. courts to handle lawsuits by foreigners against foreign officials who had violated human rights standards abroad. "Today a nation has an obligation under international law to respect the right of its citizens to be free of official torture."[36]

other private organizations. Within a year of the forma-
tion of the United Nations more than 100 groups from
all over the world and representing nearly 90 million
people were clamoring for consultative status. Most of
them were concerned with human rights.

By the time the International Bill was completed the
prime task of the private groups was already changing.
The standards were, for the most part, set. It was the
non-governmental organizations which were now, as
René Cassin noted, to "keep public opinion informed"
and "bring to the notice of members of official bodies,
national and international, numerous facts, abuses, gaps
and violations of human rights already known or, more
commonly, hidden. In this . . . role as disseminators of
information they are truly irreplaceable."[39]

A London lawyer named Peter Benenson filled this
role rather well with a single newspaper article in 1961
and unwittingly started a movement which came to circle
the globe. Armed only with quotations from the Universal Declaration and tales of government repression,
Benenson told the readers of the London *Observer* that
"in matters such as these governments are prepared to
follow only where public opinion leads."[40] A lot of
people apparently agreed with Benenson. In the flood of
letters which followed his appeal was the germ of a
group that was to win the Nobel Prize for Peace in 1977
and make enemies of every human rights violator in the
world.

By 1980 Amnesty International, stepchild of Benenson's 1961 "Appeal for Amnesty," counted more than
200,000 members and supporters in 134 countries working to safeguard the human rights of prisoners. In almost
daily barrages of news releases, pamphlets, newsletters,
books, special reports and letters to government officials
and labor, religious, political and business leaders around
the world Amnesty still lives by the advice of Peter
Benenson: "The most rapid way of bringing relief to

Prisoners of Conscience is publicity."[41] One measure of the group's effectiveness is the number of its "prisoners of conscience" that have been released, 20,000; another is the number of governments that have denounced its work—but here Amnesty doesn't bother to count.

In no small part because of Amnesty the 1970s was a decade when human rights became a household word and an international crusade. It wasn't until 1976 that *Facts on File,* one of the country's best indexes to news, gave "human rights" its own listing. The *New York Times* index for 1970, under its "Freedom and Human Rights" heading, listed less than thirty stories for the year, all in the United States. By 1979 there were, under the same heading, eighty-three references to foreign countries alone.

In 1976, working out of their home, Laurie Wiseberg and Harry M. Scoble began keeping tabs on the activities of human rights groups. Their first newsletter was fourteen pages, mimeographed. By 1980 Wiseberg and her husband were working with a full-time staff of six, their Human Rights Internet had become an international clearing house of information, and the newsletter was pushing 170 photo-offset pages. Wiseberg counts over 1,000 human rights groups in eastern and western Europe; more than 500 in North America; and 400 in the Third World—"almost all of them born after 1970," she says. "Of course there have been human rights groups around for a long time, but the whole thing just exploded in the '70s. Even groups that had never thought of human rights—church groups, political science groups, science groups—set up special human rights committees or conferences."[42]

Another watershed of human rights was marked by the election of Jimmy Carter to the U.S. presidency in 1976. Though sometimes criticized for not pursuing a consistent policy, he succeeded in making human rights a central concern of U.S. foreign relations—as well as a concern of governments which would have preferred not thinking about rights. Carter said in 1977 that "we have a right to speak out openly when we have a concern about human rights wherever those abuses occur."[43] And he did. He upgraded the head of the State Department's human rights division to an Assistant Secretary of State; he signed the International Covenants and sent them to the Senate urging ratification; he ended foreign aid to countries which violated human rights; he entertained Soviet dissidents in the White House. For almost every one of his statements or actions there was front-page newspaper coverage that spread his human rights message around the world.

"Jimmy Carter did more for human rights than any other single person in recent history," says Andreas Mavrommatis, chairman of the U.N. Human Rights Committee. "He put it in the forefront. And despite its drawbacks, his policy provided a tremendous boost in the real enjoyment of human rights."[44]

It seems one of the most intriguing characteristics of human rights that they must be demanded in order to be obtained and threatened in order to be enjoyed. Often they are not even recognized until they are gone. The Universal Declaration did not write itself. Nor were the principles, rights and freedoms which it defines—no matter how "inalienable" or "inherent" they may be—simply plucked from the air, unless it was that which rose polluted from Hitler's death camps.

"Rights are obviously part of the issues of the moment," says Gerhard Elston. "Look at our own Bill of Rights, for example. It was very specific—freedom of the press for instance—at precisely those points where the previous government was felt to be very obnoxious and oppressive. . . . Rights are what people struggle for; and they vary from place to place, from time to time."[45]

The rights included in the International Bill of Human Rights are thus the result of different types and degrees of struggle, of varying reactions to different kinds of oppression, and of demands for the fulfillment of different needs. The International Bill represents what Jimmy Carter described as "a more universal demand for fundamental human rights."[46] But if the last thirty years have taught the world anything it is that the demand must be constant and the vigil unflagging.

The next chapter in the history belongs to us.

REFERENCES

1. Eleanor Roosevelt, at a ceremony in the United Nations, New York, 27 March 1958; cited in Ethel C. Phillips, *You in Human Rights* (New York: U.S. National Commission for UNESCO, 1967), p. 2.
2. John P. Humphrey, "The U.N. Charter and the Universal Declaration of Human Rights," in *The International Protection of Human Rights,* ed. Evan Luard (New York: Frederick A. Praeger, Inc., 1967), p. 39.
3. Ibid.
4. From Article 1 of the Charter of the United Nations, signed at San Francisco 26 June 1945, entered into force 24 October 1945.
5. From Article 13, ibid.
6. From Article 68, ibid.
7. Harry S. Truman, cited in A. H. Robertson, *Human Rights in the World* (Manchester: Manchester University Press, 1972), p. 25.
8. From the Preamble to the Charter of the U.N.
9. The United Nations *Weekly Bulletin,* 17 June 1947, p. 639.
10. Ibid., pp. 639-40.
11. From the Preamble to the Charter of the U.N.
12. Franklin Delano Roosevelt, "Address to the Joint Session of Congress," 6 January 1941, in *Great Issues in American History: A Documentary Record,* vol. II, ed. Richard Hofstadter (New York: Alfred A. Knopf, Inc. 1958), Vintage Books edition, pp. 398-9.
13. René Cassin, "Madame Roosevelt que j'ai connue," in *La Pensée et L'Action* (Paris: Editions F. Lalon, 1968), p. 82.
14. All quotes from the summary of that meeting in U.N. *Weekly Bulletin,* 25 February 1947, pp. 170-71. See also "Report to the Economic and Social Council on the First Session of the Commission, Held at Lake Success, New York, from 27 January to 10 February 1947" (U.N. Document E/259).

15. *Weekly Bulletin,* ibid.
16. Humphrey, op. cit., pp. 50–51.
17. René Cassin, "La Declaration Universelle et la mise en oeuvre des droits de l'homme," in *Recueil des Cours de l'Academie de Droit International* (1951), p. 297.
18. Official records of the Third Session of the General Assembly, Part I, Plenary Meetings, 10 December 1948, pp. 923-4, 929.
19. Humphrey, p. 49.
20. Eleanor Roosevelt, cited in Robertson, op. cit., p. 27.
21. Cited in Louis B. Sohn, "A Short History of United Nations Documents on Human Rights," in *The United Nations and Human Rights,* eighteenth report of the Commission to Study the Organization of Peace (New York: 1968), p. 105.
22. U.N. Economic and Social Council (ECOSOC) Resolution 384 (XIII)C, 29 August 1951.
23. Cassin, *La Pensée et l'Action,* p. 83.
24. Thomas Buergenthal and Louis B. Sohn, *International Protection of Human Rights* (New York: Bobbs-Merrill, 1973), pp. 964-5. This fascinating reference work is a massive volume of lengthy citations from treaties, diplomatic correspondence, debates in national and international assemblies, juridical decisions, etc., as well as interesting commentary by the authors. It is a casebook of international human rights law.
25. Sohn, "A Short History," p. 136.
26. The 1974 "Declaration and Programme of Action on the Establishment of a New International Economic Order," cited in *Basic Facts about the United Nations* (New York: United Nations, 1980), p. 47. The 1977 Resolution (32/130) was adopted at the 32nd Session of the General Assembly, 105th Plenary Meeting, 16 December 1977.
27. Sohn, "A Short History," p. 107.
28. Cited in Egon Schwelb, *Human Rights and the International Community* (Chicago: 1964), p. 52.
29. "The Proclamation of Teheran" of 13 May 1968 in *Human Rights: A Compilation of International Instruments* (New York: United Nations, 1978), p. 18.
30. Cited in Schwelb, p. 48.
31. Schwelb, p. 51.
32. Cited in *Human Rights Internet Newsletter,* June-July 1980 (Washington, D.C.), p. 131.
33. Cited in Robertson, p. 52.
34. Ibid., pp. 115-6, 122.

35. "Human and People's Rights," *The Economist,* 31 January 1981, pp. 35–6.
36. Cited in *Human Rights Internet,* op. cit., p. 130.
37. Cohen, telephone interview with the author, 28 January 1981.
38. Elston, interview with the author, 26 January 1981.
39. Cited in *The United Nations and Human Rights* (New York: United Nations, 1978), p. 20.
40. The London *Observer,* 28 May 1961, p. 21.
41. Ibid.
42. Wiseberg, telephone interview with the author, 29 January 1981.
43. Jimmy Carter, cited in Daniel P. Moynihan, "The Politics of Human Rights," *Commentary,* August 1977, p. 19.
44. Mavrommatis, interview with the author, 27 January 1981.
45. Elston, op. cit.
46. Carter, speech to an unofficial meeting of the United Nations General Assembly, New York, 17 March 1977.

THE INTERNATIONAL BILL OF

HUMAN RIGHTS

UNIVERSAL DECLARATION OF HUMAN RIGHTS

PREAMBLE

WHEREAS *recognition of the inherent dignity and of the equal and inalienable rights of all members of the human family is the foundation of freedom, justice and peace in the world,*

Whereas *disregard and contempt for human rights have resulted in barbarous acts which have outraged the conscience of mankind, and the advent of a world in which human beings shall enjoy freedom of speech and belief and freedom from fear and want has been proclaimed as the highest aspiration of the common people,*

Whereas *it is essential, if man is not to be compelled to have recourse, as a last resort, to rebellion against tyranny and oppression, that human rights should be protected by the rule of law,*

Whereas *it is essential to promote the development of friendly relations between nations,*

Whereas *the peoples of the United Nations have in the Charter reaffirmed their faith in fundamental human rights, in the dignity and worth of the human person and in the equal rights of men and women and have determined to promote social progress and better standards of life in larger freedom,*

Whereas *Member States have pledged themselves to achieve, in co-operation with the United Nations, the promotion of universal respect for and observance of human rights and fundamental freedoms,*

Whereas *a common understanding of these rights and freedoms is of the greatest importance for the full realization of this pledge,*

Now, therefore, THE GENERAL ASSEMBLY *proclaims*

THIS *Universal Declaration of Human Rights as a common standard of achievement for all peoples and all nations, to the end that every individual and every organ of society, keeping this Declaration constantly in mind, shall strive by teaching and education to promote respect for these rights and freedoms and by progressive measures, national and international, to secure their universal and effective recognition and observance, both among the peoples of Member States themselves and among the peoples of territories under their jurisdiction.*

♦ *Article 1*

All human beings are born free and equal in dignity and rights. They are endowed with reason and conscience and should act towards one another in a spirit of brotherhood.

♦ *Article 2*

Everyone is entitled to all the rights and freedoms set forth in this Declaration, without distinction of any kind, such as race, colour, sex, language, religion, political or other opinion, national or social origin, property, birth or other status.

Furthermore, no distinction shall be made on the basis of the political, jurisdictional or international status of the country or territory to which a person belongs, whether it be independent, trust, non-self-governing or under any other limitation of sovereignty.

♦ *Article 3*

Everyone has the right to life, liberty and security of person.

♦ *Article 4*

No one shall be held in slavery or servitude; slavery and the slave trade shall be prohibited in all their forms.

♦ *Article 5*

No one shall be subjected to torture or to cruel, inhuman or degrading treatment or punishment.

♦ *Article 6*

Everyone has the right to recognition everywhere as a person before the law.

◆ *Article 7*

All are equal before the law and are entitled without any discrimination to equal protection of the law. All are entitled to equal protection against any discrimination in violation of this Declaration and against any incitement to such discrimination.

◆ *Article 8*

Everyone has the right to an effective remedy by the competent national tribunals for acts violating the fundamental rights granted him by the constitution or by law.

◆ *Article 9*

No one shall be subjected to arbitrary arrest, detention or exile.

◆ *Article 10*

Everyone is entitled in full equality to a fair and public hearing by an independent and impartial tribunal, in the determination of his rights and obligations and of any criminal charge against him.

◆ *Article 11*

1. Everyone charged with a penal offence has the right to be presumed innocent until proved guilty according to law in a public trial at which he has had all the guarantees necessary for his defence.

2. No one shall be held guilty of any penal offence on account of any act or omission which did not constitute a penal offence, under national or international law, at the time when it was committed. Nor shall a heavier penalty be imposed than the one that was applicable at the time the penal offence was committed.

♦ *Article 12*

No one shall be subjected to arbitrary interference with his privacy, family, home or correspondence, nor to attacks upon his honour and reputation. Everyone has the right to the protection of the law against such interference or attacks.

♦ *Article 13*

1. Everyone has the right to freedom of movement and residence within the borders of each state.

2. Everyone has the right to leave any country, including his own, and to return to his country.

♦ *Article 14*

1. Everyone has the right to seek and to enjoy in other countries asylum from persecution.

2. This right may not be invoked in the case of prosecutions genuinely arising from non-political crimes or from acts contrary to the purposes and principles of the United Nations.

♦ *Article 15*

1. Everyone has the right to a nationality.

2. No one shall be arbitrarily deprived of his nationality nor denied the right to change his nationality.

♦ *Article 16*

1. Men and women of full age, without any limitation due to race, nationality or religion, have the right to marry and to found a family. They are entitled to equal rights as to marriage, during marriage and at its dissolution.

2. Marriage shall be entered into only with the free and full consent of the intending spouses.

3. The family is the natural and fundamental group unit of society and is entitled to protection by society and the State.

♦ *Article 17*

1. Everyone has the right to own property alone as well as in association with others.

2. No one shall be arbitrarily deprived of his property.

♦ *Article 18*

Everyone has the right to freedom of thought, conscience and religion; this right includes freedom to change his religion or belief, and freedom, either alone or in community with others and in public or private, to manifest his religion or belief in teaching, practice, worship and observance.

♦ *Article 19*

Everyone has the right to freedom of opinion and expression; this right includes freedom to hold opinions without interference and to seek, receive and impart information and ideas through any media and regardless of frontiers.

♦ *Article 20*

1. Everyone has the right to freedom of peaceful assembly and association.

2. No one may be compelled to belong to an association.

♦ *Article 21*

1. Everyone has the right to take part in the government of his country, directly or through freely chosen representatives.

2. Everyone has the right of equal access to public service in his country.

3. The will of the people shall be the basis of the authority of government; this will shall be expressed in periodic and genuine elections which shall be by universal and equal suffrage and shall be held by secret vote or by equivalent free voting procedures.

♦ *Article 22*

Everyone, as a member of society, has the right to social security and is entitled to realization, through national effort and international co-operation and in accordance with the organization and resources of each State, of the economic, social and cultural rights indispensable for his dignity and the free development of his personality.

♦ *Article 23*

1. Everyone has the right to work, to free choice of employment, to just and favourable conditions of work and to protection against unemployment.

2. Everyone, without any discrimination, has the right to equal pay for equal work.

3. Everyone who works has the right to just and favourable remuneration ensuring for himself and his family an existence worthy of human dignity, and supplemented, if necessary, by other means of social protection.

4. Everyone has the right to form and to join trade unions for the protection of his interests.

♦ *Article 24*

Everyone has the right to rest and leisure, including reasonable limitation of working hours and periodic holidays with pay.

♦ *Article 25*

1. Everyone has the right to a standard of living adequate for the health and well-being of himself and of his family, including food, clothing, housing and medical care and necessary social services, and the right to security in the event of unemployment, sickness, disability,

widowhood, old age or other lack of livelihood in circumstances beyond his control.

2. Motherhood and childhood are entitled to special care and assistance. All children, whether born in or out of wedlock, shall enjoy the same social protection.

♦ *Article 26*

1. Everyone has the right to education. Education shall be free, at least in the elementary and fundamental stages. Elementary education shall be compulsory. Technical and professional education shall be made generally available and higher education shall be equally accessible to all on the basis of merit.

2. Education shall be directed to the full development of the human personality and to the strengthening of respect for human rights and fundamental freedoms. It shall promote understanding, tolerance and friendship among all nations, racial or religious groups, and shall further the activities of the United Nations for the maintenance of peace.

3. Parents have a prior right to choose the kind of education that shall be given to their children.

♦ *Article 27*

1. Everyone has the right freely to participate in the cultural life of the community, to enjoy the arts and to share in scientific advancement and its benefits.

2. Everyone has the right to the protection of the moral and material interests resulting from any scientific, literary or artistic production of which he is the author.

♦ *Article 28*

Everyone is entitled to a social and international order in which the rights and freedoms set forth in this Declaration can be fully realized.

♦ *Article 29*

1. Everyone has duties to the community in which alone the free and full development of his personality is possible.

2. In the exercise of his rights and freedoms, everyone shall be subject only to such limitations as are determined by law solely for the purpose of securing due recognition and respect for the rights and freedoms of others and of meeting the just requirements of morality, public order and the general welfare in a democratic society.

3. These rights and freedoms may in no case be exercised contrary to the purposes and principles of the United Nations.

♦ *Article 30*

Nothing in this Declaration may be interpreted as implying for any State, group or person any right to engage in any activity or to perform any act aimed at the destruction of any of the rights and freedoms set forth herein.

INTERNATIONAL COVENANT ON ECONOMIC, SOCIAL AND CULTURAL RIGHTS

PREAMBLE

The States Parties to the present Covenant,

CONSIDERING *that, in accordance with the principles proclaimed in the Charter of the United Nations, recognition of the inherent dignity and of the equal and inalienable rights of all members of the human family is the foundation of freedom, justice and peace in the world,*

Recognizing *that these rights derive from the inherent dignity of the human person,*

Recognizing *that, in accordance with the Universal Declaration of Human Rights, the ideal of free human beings enjoying freedom from fear and want can only be achieved if conditions are created whereby everyone may enjoy his economic, social and cultural rights, as well as his civil and political rights,*

Considering *the obligation of States under the Charter of the United Nations to promote universal respect for, and observance of, human rights and freedoms,*

Realizing *that the individual, having duties to other individuals and to the community to which he belongs, is under a responsibility to strive for the promotion and observance of the rights recognized in the present Covenant,*

Agree *upon the following articles:*

PART I

♦ *Article 1*

1. All peoples have the right of self-determination. By virtue of that right they freely determine their political status and freely pursue their economic, social and cultural development.

2. All peoples may, for their own ends, freely dispose of their natural wealth and resources without prejudice to any obligations arising out of international economic co-operation, based upon the principle of mutual benefit, and international law. In no case may a people be deprived of its own means of subsistence.

3. The States Parties to the present Covenant, including those having responsibility for the administration of Non-Self-Governing and Trust Territories, shall promote the realization of the right of self-determination, and shall respect that right, in conformity with the provisions of the Charter of the United Nations.

PART II

♦ *Article 2*

1. Each State Party to the present Covenant undertakes to take steps, individually and through international assistance and co-operation, especially economic and technical, to the maximum of its available resources, with a view to achieving progressively the full realization of the rights recognized in the present Covenant by all appropriate means, including

particularly the adoption of legislative measures.

2. The States Parties to the present Covenant undertake to guarantee that the rights enunciated in the present Covenant will be exercised without discrimination of any kind as to race, colour, sex, language, religion, political or other opinion, national or social origin, property, birth or other status.

3. Developing countries, with due regard to human rights and their national economy, may determine to what extent they would guarantee the economic rights recognized in the present Covenant to non-nationals.

♦ *Article 3*

The States Parties to the present Covenant undertake to ensure the equal right of men and women to the enjoyment of all economic, social and cultural rights set forth in the present Covenant.

♦ *Article 4*

The States Parties to the present Covenant recognize that, in the enjoyment of those rights provided by the State in conformity with the present Covenant, the State may subject such rights only to such limitations as are determined by law only in so far as this may be compatible with the nature of these rights and solely for the purpose of promoting the general welfare in a democratic society.

♦ *Article 5*

1. Nothing in the present Covenant may be

interpreted as implying for any State, group or person any right to engage in any activity or to perform any act aimed at the destruction of any of the rights or freedoms recognized herein, or at their limitation to a greater extent than is provided for in the present Covenant.

2. No restriction upon or derogation from any of the fundamental human rights recognized or existing in any country in virtue of law, conventions, regulations or custom shall be admitted on the pretext that the present Covenant does not recognize such rights or that it recognizes them to a lesser extent.

PART III

♦ *Article 6*

1. The States Parties to the present Covenant recognize the right to work, which includes the right of everyone to the opportunity to gain his living by work which he freely chooses or accepts, and will take appropriate steps to safeguard this right.

2. The steps to be taken by a State Party to the present Covenant to achieve the full realization of this right shall include technical and vocational guidance and training programmes, policies and techniques to achieve steady economic, social and cultural development and full and productive employment under conditions safeguarding fundamental political and economic freedoms to the individual.

♦ *Article 7*

The States Parties to the present Covenant recognize the right of everyone to the enjoyment of just and favourable conditions of work which ensure, in particular:

(a) Remuneration which provides all workers, as a minimum, with:

(i) Fair wages and equal remuneration for work of equal value without distinction of any kind, in particular women being guaranteed conditions of work not inferior to those enjoyed by men, with equal pay for equal work;

(ii) A decent living for themselves and their families in accordance with the provisions of the present Covenant;

(b) Safe and healthy working conditions;

(c) Equal opportunity for everyone to be promoted in his employment to an appropriate higher level, subject to no considerations other than those of seniority and competence;

(d) Rest, leisure and reasonable limitation of working hours and periodic holidays with pay, as well as remuneration for public holidays.

♦ *Article 8*

1. The States Parties to the present Covenant undertake to ensure:

(a) The right of everyone to form trade unions and join the trade union of his choice, subject only to the rules of the organization

concerned, for the promotion and protection of his economic and social interests. No restrictions may be placed on the exercise of this right other than those prescribed by law and which are necessary in a democratic society in the interests of national security or public order or for the protection of the rights and freedoms of others;

(b) The right of trade unions to establish national federations or confederations and the right of the latter to form or join international trade-union organizations;

(c) The right of trade unions to function freely subject to no limitations other than those prescribed by law and which are necessary in a democratic society in the interests of national security or public order or for the protection of the rights and freedoms of others;

(d) The right to strike, provided that it is exercised in conformity with the laws of the particular country;

2. This article shall not prevent the imposition of lawful restrictions on the exercise of these rights by members of the armed forces or of the police or of the administration of the State.

3. Nothing in this article shall authorize States Parties to the International Labour Organisation Convention of 1948 concerning Freedom of Association and Protection of the Right to Organize to take legislative measures which

would prejudice, or apply the law in such a manner as would prejudice, the guarantees provided for in that Convention.

♦ *Article 9*

The States Parties to the present Covenant recognize the right of everyone to social security, including social insurance.

♦ *Article 10*

The States Parties to the present Covenant recognize that:

1. The widest possible protection and assistance should be accorded to the family, which is the natural and fundamental group unit of society, particularly for its establishment and while it is responsible for the care and education of dependent children. Marriage must be entered into with the free consent of the intending spouses.

2. Special protection should be accorded to mothers during a reasonable period before and after childbirth. During such period working mothers should be accorded paid leave or leave with adequate social security benefits.

3. Special measures of protection and assistance should be taken on behalf of all children and young persons without any discrimination for reasons of parentage or other conditions. Children and young persons should be protected from economic and social exploitation.

Their employment in work harmful to their morals or health or dangerous to life or likely to hamper their normal development should be punishable by law. States should also set age limits below which the paid employment of child labour should be prohibited and punishable by law.

♦ *Article 11*

1. The States Parties to the present Covenant recognize the right of everyone to an adequate standard of living for himself and his family, including adequate food, clothing and housing, and to the continuous improvement of living conditions. The States Parties will take appropriate steps to ensure the realization of this right, recognizing to this effect the essential importance of international co-operation based on free consent.

2. The States Parties to the present Covenant, recognizing the fundamental right of everyone to be free from hunger, shall take, individually and through international co-operation, the measures, including specific programmes, which are needed:

(a) To improve methods of production, conservation and distribution of food by making full use of technical and scientific knowledge, by disseminating knowledge of the principles of nutrition and by developing or reforming agrarian systems in such a way as to achieve the most efficient development and utilization of natural resources;

(b) Taking into account the problems of both food-importing and food-exporting countries, to ensure an equitable distribution of world food supplies in relation to need.

♦ *Article 12*

1. The States Parties to the present Covenant recognize the right of everyone to the enjoyment of the highest attainable standard of physical and mental health.

2. The steps to be taken by the States Parties to the present Covenant to achieve the full realization of this right shall include those necessary for:

(a) The provision for the reduction of the stillbirth-rate and of infant mortality and for the healthy development of the child;

(b) The improvement of all aspects of environmental and industrial hygiene;

(c) The prevention, treatment and control of epidemic, endemic, occupational and other diseases;

(d) The creation of conditions which would assure to all medical service and medical attention in the event of sickness.

♦ *Article 13*

1. The States Parties to the present Covenant recognize the right of everyone to education. They agree that education shall be directed to the full development of the human personality and the sense of its dignity, and shall strengthen

the respect for human rights and fundamental freedoms. They further agree that education shall enable all persons to participate effectively in a free society, promote understanding, tolerance and friendship among all nations and all racial, ethnic or religious groups, and further the activities of the United Nations for the maintenance of peace.

2. The States Parties to the present Covenant recognize that, with a view to achieving the full realization of this right:

(a) Primary education shall be compulsory and available free to all;

(b) Secondary education in its different forms, including technical and vocational secondary education, shall be made generally available and accessible to all by every appropriate means, and in particular by the progressive introduction of free education;

(c) Higher education shall be made equally accessible to all, on the basis of capacity, by every appropriate means, and in particular by the progressive introduction of free education;

(d) Fundamental education shall be encouraged or intensified as far as possible for those persons who have not received or completed the whole period of their primary education;

(e) The development of a system of schools at all levels shall be actively pursued, an adequate fellowship system shall be established, and the material conditions of teaching staff shall be continuously improved.

3. The States Parties to the present Covenant undertake to have respect for the liberty of parents and, when applicable, legal guardians to choose for their children schools, other than those established by the public authorities, which conform to such minimum educational standards as may be laid down or approved by the State and to ensure the religious and moral education of their children in conformity with their own convictions.

4. No part of this article shall be construed so as to interfere with the liberty of individuals and bodies to establish and direct educational institutions, subject always to the observance of the principles set forth in paragraph 1 of this article and to the requirement that the education given in such institutions shall conform to such minimum standards as may be laid down by the State.

♦ *Article 14*

Each State Party to the present Covenant which, at the time of becoming a Party, has not been able to secure in its metropolitan territory or other territories under its jurisdiction compulsory primary education, free of charge, undertakes, within two years, to work out and adopt a detailed plan of action for the progressive implementation, within a reasonable number of years, to be fixed in the plan, of the principle of compulsory education free of charge for all.

♦ *Article 15*

1. The States Parties to the present Covenant recognize the right of everyone:

(a) To take part in cultural life;

(b) To enjoy the benefits of scientific progress and its applications;

(c) To benefit from the protection of the moral and material interests resulting from any scientific, literary or artistic production of which he is the author.

2. The steps to be taken by the States Parties to the present Covenant to achieve the full realization of this right shall include those necessary for the conservation, the development and the diffusion of science and culture.

3. The States Parties to the present Covenant undertake to respect the freedom indispensable for scientific research and creative activity.

4. The States Parties to the present Covenant recognize the benefits to be derived from the encouragement and development of international contacts and co-operation in the scientific and cultural fields.

PART IV

Article 16

1. The States Parties to the present Covenant undertake to submit in conformity with this part of the Covenant reports on the measures which they have adopted and the progress made in achieving the observance of the rights recognized herein.

2. *(a)* All reports shall be submitted to the Secretary-

General of the United Nations, who shall transmit copies to the Economic and Social Council for consideration in accordance with the provisions of the present Covenant.

(b) The Secretary-General of the United Nations shall also transmit to the specialized agencies copies of the reports, or any relevant parts therefrom, from States Parties to the present Covenant which are also members of these specialized agencies in so far as these reports, or parts therefrom, relate to any matters which fall within the responsibilities of the said agencies in accordance with their constitutional instruments.

Article 17

1. The States Parties to the present Covenant shall furnish their reports in stages, in accordance with a programme to be established by the Economic and Social Council within one year of the entry into force of the present Covenant after consultation with the States Parties and the specialized agencies concerned.

2. Reports may indicate factors and difficulties affecting the degree of fulfillment of obligations under the present Covenant.

3. Where relevant information has previously been furnished to the United Nations or to any specialized agency by any State Party to the present Covenant, it will not be necessary to reproduce that information, but a precise reference to the information so furnished will suffice.

Article 18

Pursuant to its responsibilities under the Charter of the United Nations in the field of human rights and fundamental freedoms, the Economic and Social Council may make arrangements with the specialized agencies in respect of their reporting to it on the progress made in achieving the observance of the provisions of the present Covenant falling within the scope of their activities. These reports may include particulars of decisions and recommendations on such implementation adopted by their competent organs.

Article 19

The Economic and Social Council may transmit to the Commission on Human Rights for study and general recommendations or, as appropriate, for information the reports concerning human rights submitted by States in accordance with articles 16 and 17, and those concerning human rights submitted by the specialized agencies in accordance with article 18.

Article 20

The States Parties to the present Covenant and the specialized agencies concerned may submit comments to the Economic and Social Council on any general recommendation under article 19 or reference to such general recommendation in any report of the Commission on Human Rights or any documentation referred to therein.

Article 21

The Economic and Social Council may submit from time to time to the General Assembly reports with recommendations of a general nature and a summary of the information received from the States Parties to the present Covenant and the specialized agencies on the measures taken and the progress made in achieving general observance of the rights recognized in the present Covenant.

Article 22

The Economic and Social Council may bring to the attention of other organs of the United Nations, their subsidiary organs and specialized agencies concerned with furnishing technical assistance any matters arising out of the reports referred to in this part of the present Covenant which may assist such bodies in deciding, each within its field of competence, on the advisability of international measures likely to contribute to the effective progressive implementation of the present Covenant.

Article 23

The States Parties to the present Covenant agree that international action for the achievement of the rights recognized in the present Covenant includes such methods as the conclusion of conventions, the adoption of recommendations, the furnishing of technical assistance and the holding of regional meetings and technical meetings for the purpose of consultation and study organized in conjunction with the Governments concerned.

Article 24

Nothing in the present Covenant shall be interpreted as impairing the provisions of the Charter of the United Nations and of the constitutions of the specialized agencies which define the respective responsibilities of the various organs of the United Nations and of the specialized agencies in regard to the matters dealt with in the present Covenant.

Article 25

Nothing in the present Covenant shall be interpreted as impairing the inherent right of all peoples to enjoy and utilize fully and freely their natural wealth and resources.

PART V

Article 26

1. The present Covenant is open for signature by any State Member of the United Nations or member of any of its specialized agencies, by any State Party to the Statute of the International Court of Justice, and by any other State which has been invited by the General Assembly of the United Nations to become a party to the present Covenant.

2. The present Covenant is subject to ratification. Instruments of ratification shall be deposited with the Secretary-General of the United Nations.

3. The present Covenant shall be open to accession by any State referred to in paragraph 1 of this article.

4. Accession shall be effected by the deposit of an instrument of accession with the Secretary-General of the United Nations.

5. The Secretary-General of the United Nations shall inform all States which have signed the present Covenant or acceded to it of the deposit of each instrument of ratification or accession.

Article 27

1. The present Covenant shall enter into force three months after the date of deposit with the Secretary-General of the United Nations of the thirty-fifth instrument of ratification or instrument of accession.

2. For each State ratifying the present Covenant or acceding to it after the deposit of the thirty-fifth instrument of ratification or instrument of accession, the present Covenant shall enter into force three months after the date of the deposit of its own instrument of ratification or instrument of accession.

Article 28

The provisions of the present Covenant shall extend to all parts of federal States without any limitations or exceptions.

Article 29

1. Any State Party to the present Covenant may propose an amendment and file it with the Secretary-General of the United Nations. The Secretary-General shall thereupon communicate any proposed amendments to the States Parties to the present Covenant with a request that they notify him whether they favour a conference of States Parties for the purpose of considering and voting upon the proposals. In the event that at least one third of the States Parties favours such a conference, the Secretary-General shall convene the conference under the auspices of the United Nations. Any amendment adopted by a majority of the States Parties present and voting at the conference shall be submitted to the General Assembly of the United Nations for approval.

2. Amendments shall come into force when they have been approved by the General Assembly of the United Nations and accepted by a two-thirds majority of the

States Parties to the present Covenant in accordance with their respective constitutional processes.

3. When amendments come into force they shall be binding on those States Parties which have accepted them, other States Parties still being bound by the provisions of the present Covenant and any earlier amendment which they have accepted.

Article 30

Irrespective of the notifications made under article 26, paragraph 5, the Secretary-General of the United Nations shall inform all States referred to in paragraph 1 of the same article of the following particulars:

(a) Signatures, ratifications and accessions under article 26;

(b) The date of the entry into force of the present Covenant under article 27 and the date of the entry into force of any amendments under article 29.

Article 31

1. The present Covenant, of which the Chinese, English, French, Russian and Spanish texts are equally authentic, shall be deposited in the archives of the United Nations.

2. The Secretary-General of the United Nations shall transmit certified copies of the present Covenant to all States referred to in article 26.

INTERNATIONAL COVENANT ON CIVIL AND POLITICAL RIGHTS

PREAMBLE

The States Parties to the present Covenant,

CONSIDERING *that, in accordance with the principles proclaimed in the Charter of the United Nations, recognition of the inherent dignity and of the equal and inalienable rights of all members of the human family is the foundation of freedom, justice and peace in the world,*

Recognizing *that these rights derive from the inherent dignity of the human person,*

Recognizing *that, in accordance with the Universal Declaration of Human Rights, the ideal of free human beings enjoying civil and political freedom and freedom from fear and want can only be achieved if conditions are created whereby everyone may enjoy his civil and political rights, as well as his economic, social and cultural rights,*

Considering *the obligations of States under the Charter of the United Nations to promote universal respect for, and observance of, human rights and freedoms,*

Realizing *that the individual, having duties to other individuals and to the community to which he belongs, is under a responsibility to*

strive for the promotion and observance of the rights recognized in the present Covenant,
  Agree *upon the following articles:*

PART I

♦ *Article 1*

  1. All peoples have the right of self-determination. By virtue of that right they freely determine their political status and freely pursue their economic, social and cultural development.

  2. All peoples may, for their own ends, freely dispose of their natural wealth and resources without prejudice to any obligations arising out of international economic co-operation, based upon the principle of mutual benefit, and international law. In no case may a people be deprived of its own means of subsistence.

  3. The States Parties to the present Covenant, including those having responsibility for the administration of Non-Self-Governing and Trust Territories, shall promote the realization of the right of self-determination, and shall respect that right, in conformity with the provisions of the Charter of the United Nations.

PART II

♦ *Article 2*

  1. Each State Party to the present Covenant

undertakes to respect and to ensure to all individuals within its territory and subject to its jurisdiction the rights recognized in the present Covenant, without distinction of any kind, such as race, colour, sex, language, religion, political or other opinion, national or social origin, property, birth or other status.

2. Where not already provided for by existing legislative or other measures, each State Party to the present Covenant undertakes to take the necessary steps, in accordance with its constitutional processes and with the provisions of the present Covenant, to adopt such legislative or other measures as may be necessary to give effect to the rights recognized in the present Covenant.

3. Each State Party to the present Covenant undertakes:

(a) To ensure that any person whose rights or freedoms as herein recognized are violated shall have an effective remedy, notwithstanding that the violation has been committed by persons acting in an official capacity;

(b) To ensure that any person claiming such a remedy shall have his right thereto determined by competent judicial, administrative or legislative authorities, or by any other competent authority provided for by the legal system of the State, and to develop the possibilities of judicial remedy;

(c) To ensure that the competent authorities shall enforce such remedies when granted.

♦ *Article 3*

The States Parties to the present Covenant undertake to ensure the equal right of men and women to the enjoyment of all civil and political rights set forth in the present Covenant.

♦ *Article 4*

1. In time of public emergency which threatens the life of the nation and the existence of which is officially proclaimed, the States Parties to the present Covenant may take measures derogating from their obligations under the present Covenant to the extent strictly required by the exigencies of the situation, provided that such measures are not inconsistent with their other obligations under international law and do not involve discrimination solely on the ground of race, colour, sex, language, religion or social origin.

2. No derogation from articles 6, 7, 8 (paragraphs 1 and 2), 11, 15, 16 and 18 may be made under this provision.

3. Any State Party to the present Covenant availing itself of the right of derogation shall immediately inform the other States Parties to the present Covenant, through the intermediary of the Secretary-General of the United Nations, of the provisions from which it has derogated and of the reasons by which it was actuated. A further communication shall be made, through the same intermediary, on the date on which it terminates such derogation.

♦ *Article 5*

1. Nothing in the present Covenant may be interpreted as implying for any State, group or person any right to engage in any activity or perform any act aimed at the destruction of any of the rights and freedoms recognized herein or at their limitation to a greater extent than is provided for in the present Covenant.

2. There shall be no restriction upon or derogation from any of the fundamental human rights recognized or existing in any State Party to the present Covenant pursuant to law, conventions, regulations or custom on the pretext that the present Covenant does not recognize such rights or that it recognizes them to a lesser extent.

PART III

♦ *Article 6*

1. Every human being has the inherent right to life. This right shall be protected by law. No one shall be arbitrarily deprived of his life.

2. In countries which have not abolished the death penalty, sentence of death may be imposed only for the most serious crimes in accordance with the law in force at the time of the commission of the crime and not contrary to the provisions of the present Covenant and to the Convention on the Prevention and Punishment of the Crime of Genocide. This penalty can only be carried out pursuant to a final judgment rendered by a competent court.

3. When deprivation of life constitutes the crime of genocide, it is understood that nothing in this article shall authorize any State Party to the present Covenant to derogate in any way from any obligation assumed under the provisions of the Convention on the Prevention and Punishment of the Crime of Genocide.

4. Anyone sentenced to death shall have the right to seek pardon or commutation of the sentence. Amnesty, pardon or commutation of the sentence of death may be granted in all cases.

5. Sentence of death shall not be imposed for crimes committed by persons below eighteen years of age and shall not be carried out on pregnant women.

6. Nothing in this article shall be invoked to delay or to prevent the abolition of capital punishment by any State Party to the present Covenant.

◆ *Article 7*

No one shall be subjected to torture or to cruel, inhuman or degrading treatment or punishment. In particular, no one shall be subjected without his free consent to medical or scientific experimentation.

◆ *Article 8*

1. No one shall be held in slavery: slavery and the slave-trade in all their forms shall be prohibited.

2. No one shall be held in servitude.

3. *(a)* No one shall be required to perform forced or compulsory labour.

(b) Paragraph 3 *(a)* shall not be held to preclude, in countries where imprisonment with hard labour may be imposed as a punishment for a crime, the performance of hard labour in pursuance of a sentence to such punishment by a competent court;

(c) For the purpose of this paragraph the term "forced or compulsory labour" shall not include:

(i) Any work or service, not referred to in sub-paragraph *(b),* normally required of a person who is under detention in consequence of a lawful order of a court, or of a person during conditional release from such detention;

(ii) Any service of a military character and, in countries where conscientious objection is recognized, any national service required by law of conscientious objectors;

(iii) Any service exacted in cases of emergency or calamity threatening the life or well-being of the community;

(iv) Any work or service which forms part of normal civil obligations.

♦ *Article 9*

1. Everyone has the right to liberty and security of person. No one shall be subjected to arbitrary arrest or detention. No one shall be deprived of his liberty except on such grounds and in

accordance with such procedure as are established by law.

2. Anyone who is arrested shall be informed, at the time of arrest, of the reasons for his arrest and shall be promptly informed of any charges against him.

3. Anyone arrested or detained on a criminal charge shall be brought promptly before a judge or other officer authorized by law to exercise judicial power and shall be entitled to trial within a reasonable time or to release. It shall not be the general rule that persons awaiting trial shall be detained in custody, but release may be subject to guarantees to appear for trial, at any other stage of the judicial proceedings, and, should occasion arise, for execution of the judgment.

4. Anyone who is deprived of his liberty by arrest or detention shall be entitled to take proceedings before a court, in order that that court may decide without delay on the lawfulness of his detention and order his release if the detention is not lawful.

5. Anyone who has been the victim of unlawful arrest or detention shall have an enforceable right to compensation.

♦ *Article 10*

1. All persons deprived of their liberty shall be treated with humanity and with respect for the inherent dignity of the human person.

2. *(a)* Accused persons shall, save in excep-

tional circumstances, be segregated from convicted persons and shall be subject to separate treatment appropriate to their status as unconvicted persons;

(b) Accused juvenile persons shall be separated from adults and brought as speedily as possible for adjudication.

3. The penitentiary system shall comprise treatment of prisoners the essential aim of which shall be their reformation and social rehabilitation. Juvenile offenders shall be segregated from adults and be accorded treatment appropriate to their age and legal status.

♦ *Article 11*

No one shall be imprisoned merely on the grounds of inability to fulfil a contractual obligation.

♦ *Article 12*

1. Everyone lawfully within the territory of a State shall, within that territory, have the right to liberty of movement and freedom to choose his residence.

2. Everyone shall be free to leave any country, including his own.

3. The above-mentioned rights shall not be subject to any restrictions except those which are provided by law, are necessary to protect national security, public order *(ordre public),* public health or morals or the rights and freedoms of others, and are consistent with the

other rights recognized in the present Covenant.

4. No one shall be arbitrarily deprived of the right to enter his own country.

♦ *Article 13*

An alien lawfully in the territory of a State Party to the present Covenant may be expelled therefrom only in pursuance of a decision reached in accordance with law and shall, except where compelling reasons of national security otherwise require, be allowed to submit the reasons against his expulsion and to have his case reviewed by, and be represented for the purpose before, the competent authority or a person or persons especially designated by the competent authority.

♦ *Article 14*

1. All persons shall be equal before the courts and tribunals. In the determination of any criminal charge against him, or of his rights and obligations in a suit at law, everyone shall be entitled to a fair and public hearing by a competent, independent and impartial tribunal established by law. The Press and the public may be excluded from all or part of a trial for reasons of morals, public order *(ordre public)* or national security in a democratic society, or when the interest of the private lives of the parties so requires, or to the extent strictly necessary in the opinion of the court in special circumstances where publicity would prejudice the interests of justice;

but any judgment rendered in a criminal case or in a suit at law shall be made public except where the interest of juvenile persons otherwise requires or the proceedings concern matrimonial disputes or the guardianship of children.

2. Everyone charged with a criminal offence shall have the right to be presumed innocent until proved guilty according to law.

3. In the determination of any criminal charge against him, everyone shall be entitled to the following minimum guarantees, in full equality:

   (a) To be informed promptly and in detail in language which he understands of the nature and cause of the charge against him;

   (b) To have adequate time and facilities for the preparation of his defence and to communicate with counsel of his own choosing;

   (c) To be tried without undue delay;

   (d) To be tried in his presence, and to defend himself in person or through legal assistance of his own choosing; to be informed, if he does not have legal assistance, of this right; and to have legal assistance assigned to him, in any case where the interests of justice so require, and without payment by him in any such case if he does not have sufficient means to pay for it;

   (e) To examine, or have examined, the witnesses against him and to obtain the attendance and examination of witnesses on his behalf under the same conditions as witnesses against him;

(f) To have the free assistance of an interpreter if he cannot understand or speak the language used in court;

(g) Not to be compelled to testify against himself or to confess guilt.

4. In the case of juvenile persons, the procedure shall be such as will take account of their age and the desirability of promoting their rehabilitation.

5. Everyone convicted of a crime shall have the right to his conviction and sentence being reviewed by a higher tribunal according to law.

6. When a person has by a final decision been convicted of a criminal offence and when subsequently his conviction has been reversed or he has been pardoned on the ground that a new or newly discovered fact shows conclusively that there has been a miscarriage of justice, the person who has suffered punishment as a result of such conviction shall be compensated according to law, unless it is proved that the non-disclosure of the unknown fact in time is wholly or partly attributable to him.

7. No one shall be liable to be tried or punished again for an offence for which he has already been finally convicted or acquitted in accordance with the law and penal procedure of each country.

♦ *Article 15*

1. No one shall be held guilty of any criminal offence on account of any act or omission which

did not constitute a criminal offence, under national or international law, at the time when it was committed. Nor shall a heavier penalty be imposed than the one that was applicable at the time when the criminal offence was committed. If, subsequent to the commission of the offence, provision is made by law for the imposition of a lighter penalty, the offender shall benefit thereby.

2. Nothing in this article shall prejudice the trial and punishment of any person for any act or omission which, at the time when it was committed, was criminal according to the general principles of law recognized by the community of nations.

♦ *Article 16*

Everyone shall have the right to recognition everywhere as a person before the law.

♦ *Article 17*

1. No one shall be subjected to arbitrary or unlawful interference with his privacy, family, home or correspondence, nor to unlawful attacks on his honour and reputation.

2. Everyone has the right to the protection of the law against such interference or attacks.

♦ *Article 18*

1. Everyone shall have the right to freedom of thought, conscience and religion. This right shall include freedom to have or to adopt a religion or belief of his choice, and freedom, either

individually or in community with others and in public or private, to manifest his religion or belief in worship, observance, practice and teaching.

2. No one shall be subject to coercion which would impair his freedom to have or to adopt a religion or belief of his choice.

3. Freedom to manifest one's religion or beliefs may be subject only to such limitations as are prescribed by law and are necessary to protect public safety, order, health, or morals or the fundamental rights and freedoms of others.

4. The States Parties to the present Covenant undertake to have respect for the liberty of parents and, when applicable, legal guardians to ensure the religious and moral education of their children in conformity with their own convictions.

♦ *Article 19*

1. Everyone shall have the right to hold opinions without interference.

2. Everyone shall have the right to freedom of expression; this right shall include freedom to seek, receive and impart information and ideas of all kinds, regardless of frontiers, either orally, in writing or in print, in the form of art, or through any other media of his choice.

3. The exercise of the rights provided for in paragraph 2 of this article carries with it special duties and responsibilities. It may therefore be subject to certain restrictions, but these shall

only be such as are provided by law and are necessary:

(a) For respect of the rights or reputations of others;

(b) For the protection of national security or of public order *(ordre public)*, or of public health or morals.

♦ *Article 20*

1. Any propaganda for war shall be prohibited by law.

2. Any advocacy of national, racial or religious hatred that constitutes incitement to discrimination, hostility or violence shall be prohibited by law.

♦ *Article 21*

The right of peaceful assembly shall be recognized. No restrictions may be placed on the exercise of this right other than those imposed in conformity with the law and which are necessary in a democratic society in the interests of national security or public safety, public order *(ordre public)*, the protection of public health or morals or the protection of the rights and freedoms of others.

♦ *Article 22*

1. Everyone shall have the right to freedom of association with others, including the right to form and join trade unions for the protection of his interests.

2. No restrictions may be placed on the exercise of this right other than those which are prescribed by law and which are necessary in a democratic society in the interests of national security or public safety, public order *(ordre public)*, the protection of public health or morals or the protection of the rights and freedoms of others. This article shall not prevent the imposition of lawful restrictions on members of the armed forces and of the police in their exercise of this right.

3. Nothing in this article shall authorize States Parties to the International Labour Organisation Convention of 1948 concerning Freedom of Association and Protection of the Right to Organize to take legislative measures which would prejudice, or to apply the law in such a manner as to prejudice, the guarantees provided for in that Convention.

♦ *Article 23*

1. The family is the natural and fundamental group unit of society and is entitled to protection by society and the State.

2. The right of men and women of marriageable age to marry and to found a family shall be recognized.

3. No marriage shall be entered into without the free and full consent of the intending spouses.

4. States Parties to the present Covenant shall take appropriate steps to ensure equality of

rights and responsibilities of spouses as to marriage, during marriage and at its dissolution. In the case of dissolution, provision shall be made for the necessary protection of any children.

♦ *Article 24*

1. Every child shall have, without any discrimination as to race, colour, sex, language, religion, national or social origin, property or birth, the right to such measures of protection as are required by his status as a minor, on the part of his family, society and the State.

2. Every child shall be registered immediately after birth and shall have a name.

3. Every child has the right to acquire a nationality.

♦ *Article 25*

Every citizen shall have the right and the opportunity, without any of the distinctions mentioned in article 2 and without unreasonable restrictions:

(a) To take part in the conduct of public affairs, directly or through freely chosen representatives;

(b) To vote and to be elected at genuine periodic elections which shall be by universal and equal suffrage and shall be held by secret ballot, guaranteeing the free expression of the will of the electors;

(c) To have access, on general terms of equality, to public service in his country.

♦ *Article 26*

All persons are equal before the law and are entitled without any discrimination to the equal protection of the law. In this respect, the law shall prohibit any discrimination and guarantee to all persons equal and effective protection against discrimination on any ground such as race, colour, sex, language, religion, political or other opinion, national or social origin, property, birth or other status.

♦ *Article 27*

In those States in which ethnic, religious or linguistic minorities exist, persons belonging to such minorities shall not be denied the right, in community with the other members of their group, to enjoy their own culture, to profess and practice their own religion, or to use their own language.

PART IV

Article 28

1. There shall be established a Human Rights Committee (hereafter referred to in the present Covenant as the Committee). It shall consist of eighteen members and shall carry out the functions hereinafter provided.

2. The Committee shall be composed of nationals of the States Parties to the present Covenant who shall be persons of high moral character and recognized competence in the field of human rights, consideration being given to the usefulness of the participation of some persons having legal experience.

3. The members of the Committee shall be elected and shall serve in their personal capacity.

Article 29

1. The members of the Committee shall be elected by secret ballot from a list of persons possessing the qualifications prescribed in article 28 and nominated for the purpose by the States Parties to the present Covenant.

2. Each State Party to the present Covenant may nominate not more than two persons. These persons shall be nationals of the nominating State.

3. A person shall be eligible for renomination.

Article 30

1. The initial election shall be held no later than six months after the date of the entry into force of the present Covenant.

2. At least four months before the date of each election to the Committee, other than an election to fill a vacancy declared in accordance with article 34, the Secretary-General of the United Nations shall address a written invitation to the States Parties to the present Covenant to submit their nominations for membership of the Committee within three months.

3. The Secretary-General of the United Nations shall prepare a list in alphabetical order of all the persons thus nominated, with an indication of the States Parties which have nominated them, and shall submit it to the States Parties to the present Covenant no later than one month before the date of each election.

4. Elections of the members of the Committee shall be held at a meeting of the States Parties to the present Covenant convened by the Secretary-General of the United Nations at the Headquarters of the United Nations. At that meeting, for which two thirds of the States Parties to the present Covenant shall constitute a quorum, the persons elected to the Committee shall be those nominees who obtain the largest number of votes and an absolute majority of the votes of the representatives of States Parties present and voting.

Article 31

1. The Committee may not include more than one national of the same State.

2. In the election of the Committee, consideration shall be given to equitable geographical distribution of membership and to the representation of the different forms of civilization and of the principal legal systems.

Article 32

1. The members of the Committee shall be elected for a term of four years. They shall be eligible for re-election if renominated. However, the terms of nine of the members elected at the first election shall expire at the end of two years; immediately after the first election, the names of these nine members shall be chosen by lot by the Chairman of the meeting referred to in article 30, paragraph 4.

2. Elections at the expiry of office shall be held in accordance with the preceding articles of this part of the present Covenant.

Article 33

1. If, in the unanimous opinion of the other members, a member of the Committee has ceased to carry out his functions for any cause other than absence of a temporary character, the Chairman of the Committee shall notify the Secretary-General of the United Nations, who shall then declare the seat of that member to be vacant.

2. In the event of the death or the resignation of a member of the Committee, the Chairman shall immediately notify the Secretary-General of the United Nations, who shall declare the seat vacant from the date of death or the date on which the resignation takes effect.

Article 34

1. When a vacancy is declared in accordance with article 33 and if the term of office of the member to be replaced does not expire within six months of the declaration of the vacancy, the Secretary-General of the United Nations shall notify each of the States Parties to the present Covenant, which may within two months submit nominations in accordance with article 29 for the purpose of filling the vacancy.

2. The Secretary-General of the United Nations shall prepare a list in alphabetical order of the persons thus nominated and shall submit it to the States Parties to the present Covenant. The election to fill the vacancy shall then take place in accordance with the relevant provisions of this part of the present Covenant.

3. A member of the Committee elected to fill a vacancy declared in accordance with article 33 shall hold office for the remainder of the term of the member who vacated the seat on the Committee under the provisions of that article.

Article 35

The members of the Committee shall, with the approval of the General Assembly of the United Nations, receive emoluments from United Nations resources on such terms and conditions as the General Assembly may decide, having regard to the importance of the Committee's responsibilities.

Article 36

The Secretary-General of the United Nations shall provide the necessary staff and facilities for the effective performance of the functions of the Committee under the present Covenant.

Article 37

1. The Secretary-General of the United Nations shall convene the initial meeting of the Committee at the Headquarters of the United Nations.

2. After its initial meeting, the Committee shall meet at such times as shall be provided in its rules of procedure.

3. The Committee shall normally meet at the Headquarters of the United Nations or at the United Nations Office at Geneva.

Article 38

Every member of the Committee shall, before taking up his duties, make a solemn declaration in open committee that he will perform his functions impartially and conscientiously.

Article 39

1. The Committee shall elect its officers for a term of two years. They may be re-elected.

2. The Committee shall establish its own rules of procedure, but these rules shall provide, *inter alia,* that:

(a) Twelve members shall constitute a quorum;

(b) Decisions of the Committee shall be made by a majority vote of the members present.

Article 40

1. The States Parties to the present Covenant undertake to submit reports on the measures they have adopted which give effect to the rights recognized herein and on the progress made in the enjoyment of these rights:

(a) Within one year of the entry into force of the present Covenant for the States Parties concerned;

(b) Thereafter whenever the Committee so requests.

2. All reports shall be submitted to the Secretary-General of the United Nations, who shall transmit them to the Committee for consideration. Reports shall indicate the factors and difficulties, if any, affecting the implementation of the present Covenant.

3. The Secretary-General of the United Nations may, after consultation with the Committee, transmit to the specialized agencies concerned copies of such parts of the reports as may fall within their field of competence.

4. The Committee shall study the reports submitted by the States Parties to the present Covenant. It shall transmit its reports, and such general comments as it may consider appropriate, to the States Parties. The Committee may also transmit to the Economic and Social Council these comments along with the copies of the reports it has received from States Parties to the present Covenant.

5. The States Parties to the present Covenant may submit to the Committee observations on any comments that may be made in accordance with paragraph 4 of this article.

Article 41

1. A State Party to the present Covenant may at any

time declare under this article that it recognizes the competence of the Committee to receive and consider communications to the effect that a State Party claims that another State Party is not fulfilling its obligations under the present Covenant. Communications under this article may be received and considered only if submitted by a State Party which has made a declaration recognizing in regard to itself the competence of the Committee. No communication shall be received by the Committee if it concerns a State Party which has not made such a declaration. Communications received under this article shall be dealt with in accordance with the following procedure:

(a) If a State Party to the present Covenant considers that another State Party is not giving effect to the provisions of the present Covenant, it may, by written communication, bring the matter to the attention of that State Party. Within three months after the receipt of the communication, the receiving State shall afford the State which sent the communication an explanation or any other statement in writing clarifying the matter, which should include, to the extent possible and pertinent, reference to domestic procedures and remedies taken, pending, or available in the matter.

(b) If the matter is not adjusted to the satisfaction of both States Parties concerned within six months after the receipt by the receiving State of the initial communication, either State shall have the right to refer the matter to the Committee, by notice given to the Committee and to the other State.

(c) The Committee shall deal with the matter referred to it only after it has ascertained that all available domestic remedies have been invoked and exhausted in the matter, in conformity with the generally recognized principles of international law. This shall not be the rule where the application of the remedies is unreasonably prolonged.

(d) The Committee shall hold closed meetings when examining communications under this article.

(e) Subject to the provisions of sub-paragraph (c), the

Committee shall make available its good offices to the States Parties concerned with a view to a friendly solution of the matter on the basis of respect for human rights and fundamental freedoms as recognized in the present Covenant.

(f) In any matter referred to it, the Committee may call upon the States Parties concerned, referred to in sub-paragraph *(b)*, to supply any relevant information.

(g) The States Parties concerned, referred to in subparagraph *(b)*, shall have the right to be represented when the matter is being considered in the Committee and to make submissions orally and/or in writing.

(h) The Committee shall, within twelve months after the date of receipt of notice under sub-paragraph *(b)*, submit a report:

(i) If a solution within the terms of sub-paragraph *(e)* is reached, the Committee shall confine its report to a brief statement of the facts and of the solution reached;

(ii) If a solution within the terms of sub-paragraph *(e)* is not reached, the Committee shall confine its report to a brief statement of the facts; the written submissions and record of the oral submissions made by the States Parties concerned shall be attached to the report.

In every matter, the report shall be communicated to the States Parties concerned.

2. The provisions of this article shall come into force when ten States Parties to the present Covenant have made declarations under paragraph 1 of this article. Such declarations shall be deposited by the States Parties with the Secretary-General of the United Nations, who shall transmit copies thereof to the other States Parties. A declaration may be withdrawn at any time by notification to the Secretary-General. Such a withdrawal shall not prejudice the consideration of any matter which is the subject of a communication already transmitted under this article; no further communication by any State Party shall be received after the notification of withdrawal of the declaration has been received by the Secretary-General, unless the State Party concerned has made a new declaration.

Article 42

1. *(a)* If a matter referred to the Committee in accordance with article 41 is not resolved to the satisfaction of the States Parties concerned, the Committee may, with the prior consent of the States Parties concerned, appoint an *ad hoc* Conciliation Commission (hereinafter referred to as the Commission). The good offices of the Commission shall be made available to the States Parties concerned with a view to an amicable solution of the matter on the basis of respect for the present Covenant;

(b) The Commission shall consist of five persons acceptable to the States Parties concerned. If the States Parties concerned fail to reach agreement within three months on all or part of the composition of the Commission, the members of the Commission concerning whom no agreement has been reached shall be elected by secret ballot by a two-thirds majority vote of the Committee from among its members.

2. The members of the Commission shall serve in their personal capacity. They shall not be nationals of the States Parties concerned, or of a State not party to the present Covenant, or of a State Party which has not made a declaration under article 41.

3. The Commission shall elect its own Chairman and adopt its own rules of procedure.

4. The meetings of the Commission shall normally be held at the Headquarters of the United Nations or at the United Nations Office at Geneva. However, they may be held at such other convenient places as the Commission may determine in consultation with the Secretary-General of the United Nations and the States Parties concerned.

5. The secretariat provided in accordance with article 36 shall also service the commissions appointed under this article.

6. The information received and collated by the Committee shall be made available to the Commission and the Commission may call upon the States Parties concerned to supply any other relevant information.

7. When the Commission has fully considered the matter, but in any event not later than twelve months after having been seized of the matter, it shall submit to the Chairman of the Committee a report for communication to the States Parties concerned:

(a) If the Commission is unable to complete its consideration of the matter within twelve months, it shall confine its report to a brief statement of the status of its consideration of the matter;

(b) If an amicable solution to the matter on the basis of respect for human rights as recognized in the present Covenant is reached, the Commission shall confine its report to a brief statement of the facts and of the solution reached;

(c) If a solution within the terms of sub-paragraph *(b)* is not reached, the Commission's report shall embody its findings on all questions of fact relevant to the issues between the States Parties concerned, and its views on the possibilities of an amicable solution of the matter. This report shall also contain the written submissions and a record of the oral submissions made by the States Parties concerned;

(d) If the Commission's report is submitted under sub-paragraph *(c)*, the States Parties concerned shall, within three months of the receipt of the report, notify the Chairman of the Committee whether or not they accept the contents of the report of the Commission.

8. The provisions of this article are without prejudice to the responsibilities of the Committee under article 41.

9. The States Parties concerned shall share equally all the expenses of the members of the Commission in accordance with estimates to be provided by the Secretary-General of the United Nations.

10. The Secretary-General of the United Nations shall be empowered to pay the expenses of the members of the Commission, if necessary, before reimbursement by the States Parties concerned, in accordance with paragraph 9 of this article.

Article 43

The members of the Committee, and of the *ad hoc* conciliation commissions which may be appointed under article 42, shall be entitled to the facilities, privileges and immunities of experts on mission for the United Nations as laid down in the relevant sections of the Convention on the Privileges and Immunities of the United Nations.

Article 44

The provisions for the implementation of the present Covenant shall apply without prejudice to the procedures prescribed in the field of human rights by or under the constituent instruments and the conventions of the United Nations and of the specialized agencies and shall not prevent the States Parties to the present Covenant from having recourse to other procedures for settling a dispute in accordance with general or special international agreements in force between them.

Article 45

The Committee shall submit to the General Assembly of the United Nations, through the Economic and Social Council, an annual report on its activities.

PART V

Article 46

Nothing in the present Covenant shall be interpreted as impairing the provisions of the Charter of the United Nations and of the constitutions of the specialized agencies which define the respective responsibilities of the various organs of the United Nations and of the specialized agencies in regard to the matters dealt with in the present Covenant.

Article 47

Nothing in the present Covenant shall be interpreted as impairing the inherent right of all peoples to enjoy and utilize fully and freely their natural wealth and resources.

PART VI

Article 48

1. The present Covenant is open for signature by any State Member of the United Nations or member of any of its specialized agencies, by any State Party to the Statute of the International Court of Justice, and by any other State which has been invited by the General Assembly of the United Nations to become a party to the present Covenant.

2. The present Covenant is subject to ratification. Instruments of ratification shall be deposited with the Secretary-General of the United Nations.

3. The present Covenant shall be open to accession by any State referred to in paragraph 1 of this article.

4. Accession shall be effected by the deposit of an instrument of accession with the Secretary-General of the United Nations.

5. The Secretary-General of the United Nations shall inform all States which have signed this Covenant or acceded to it of the deposit of each instrument of ratification or accession.

Article 49

1. The present Covenant shall enter into force three months after the date of the deposit with the Secretary-General of the United Nations of the thirty-fifth instrument of ratification or instrument of accession.

2. For each State ratifying the present Covenant or acceding to it after the deposit of the thirty-fifth instrument of ratification or instrument of accession, the present Covenant shall enter into force three months after the date of the deposit of its own instrument of ratification or instrument of accession.

Article 50

The provisions of the present Covenant shall extend to all parts of federal States without any limitations or exceptions.

Article 51

1. Any State Party to the present Covenant may propose an amendment and file it with the Secretary-General of the United Nations. The Secretary-General of the United Nations shall thereupon communicate any proposed amendments to the States Parties to the present Covenant with a request that they notify him whether they favour a conference of States Parties for the purpose of considering and voting upon the proposals. In the event that at least one third of the States Parties favours such a conference, the Secretary-General shall convene the conference under the auspices of the United Nations. Any amendment adopted by a majority of the States Parties present and voting at the conference shall be submitted to the General Assembly of the United Nations for approval.

2. Amendments shall come into force when they have been approved by the General Assembly of the United Nations and accepted by a two-thirds majority of the States Parties to the present Covenant in accordance with their respective constitutional processes.

3. When amendments come into force, they shall be binding on those States Parties which have accepted them, other States Parties still being bound by the provisions of the present Covenant and any earlier amendment which they have accepted.

Article 52

Irrespective of the notifications made under article 48, paragraph 5, the Secretary-General of the United Nations shall inform all States referred to in paragraph 1 of the same article of the following particulars:

(a) Signatures, ratifications and accessions under article 48;

(b) The date of the entry into force of the present Covenant under article 49 and the date of the entry into force of any amendments under article 51.

Article 53

1. The present Covenant, of which the Chinese,

English, French, Russian and Spanish texts are equally authentic, shall be deposited in the archives of the United Nations.

2. The Secretary-General of the United Nations shall transmit certified copies of the present Covenant to all States referred to in article 48.

OPTIONAL PROTOCOL TO THE INTERNATIONAL COVENANT ON CIVIL AND POLITICAL RIGHTS

The States Parties to the present Protocol,

CONSIDERING *that in order further to achieve the purposes of the Covenant on Civil and Political Rights (hereinafter referred to as the Covenant) and the implementation of its provisions it would be appropriate to enable the Human Rights Committee set up in part IV of the Covenant (hereinafter referred to as the Committee) to receive and consider, as provided in the present Protocol, communications from individuals claiming to be victims of violations of any of the rights set forth in the Covenant,*

Have agreed *as follows:*

Article 1

A State Party to the Covenant that becomes a party to the present Protocol recognizes the competence of the Committee to receive and consider communications from individuals subject to its jurisdiction who claim to be victims of a violation by that State Party of any of the rights set forth in the Covenant. No communication shall be received by the Committee if it concerns a State Party to the Covenant which is not a party to the present Protocol.

Article 2

Subject to the provisions of article 1, individuals who claim that any of their rights enumerated in the Covenant have been violated and who have exhausted all available domestic remedies may submit a written communication to the Committee for consideration.

Article 3

The Committee shall consider inadmissible any communication under the present Protocol which is anonymous, or which it considers to be an abuse of the rights of submission of such communications or to be incompatible with the provisions of the Covenant.

Article 4

1. Subject to the provisions of article 3, the Committee shall bring any communications submitted to it under the present Protocol to the attention of the State Party to the present Protocol alleged to be violating any provisions of the Covenant.

2. Within six months, the receiving State shall submit to the Committee written explanations or statements clarifying the matter and the remedy, if any, that may have been taken by that State.

Article 5

1. The Committee shall consider communications received under the present Protocol in the light of all written information made available to it by the individual and by the State Party concerned.

2. The Committee shall not consider any communication from an individual unless it has ascertained that:

(a) The same matter is not being examined under another procedure of international investigation or settlement;

(b) The individual has exhausted all available domestic remedies. This shall not be the rule where the application of the remedies is unreasonably prolonged.

3. The Committee shall hold closed meetings when examining communications under the present Protocol.

4. The Committee shall forward its views to the State Party concerned and to the individual.

Article 6

The Committee shall include in its annual report under article 45 of the Covenant a summary of its activities under the present Protocol.

Article 7

Pending the achievement of the objectives of resolution 1514 (XV) adopted by the General Assembly of the United Nations on 14 December 1960 concerning the Declaration on the Granting of Independence to Colonial Countries and Peoples, the provisions of the present Protocol shall in no way limit the right of petition granted to these peoples by the Charter of the United Nations and other international conventions and instruments under the United Nations and its specialized agencies.

Article 8

1. The present Protocol is open for signature by any State which has signed the Covenant.

2. The present Protocol is subject to ratification by any State which has ratified or acceded to the Covenant. Instruments of ratification shall be deposited with the Secretary-General of the United Nations.

3. The present Protocol shall be open to accession by any State which has ratified or acceded to the Covenant.

4. Accession shall be effected by the deposit of an instrument of accession with the Secretary-General of the United Nations.

5. The Secretary-General of the United Nations shall inform all States which have signed the present Protocol or acceded to it of the deposit of each instrument of ratification or accession.

Article 9

1. Subject to the entry into force of the Covenant, the present Protocol shall enter into force three months after the date of the deposit with the Secretary-General of the United Nations of the tenth instrument of ratification or instrument of accession.

2. For each State ratifying the present Protocol or acceding to it after the deposit of the tenth instrument of ratification or instrument of accession, the present Protocol shall enter into force three months after the date of the deposit of its own instrument of ratification or instrument of accession.

Article 10

The provisions of the present Protocol shall extend to all parts of federal States without any limitations or exceptions.

Article 11

1. Any State Party to the present Protocol may propose an amendment and file it with the Secretary-General of the United Nations. The Secretary-General shall thereupon communicate any proposed amendments to the States Parties to the present Protocol with a request that they notify him whether they favour a conference of States Parties for the purpose of considering and voting upon the proposal. In the event that at least one third of the States Parties favours such a conference, the Secretary-General shall convene the conference under the auspices of the United Nations. Any amendment adopted by a majority of the States Parties present and voting at the conference shall be submitted to the General Assembly of the United Nations for approval.

2. Amendments shall come into force when they have been approved by the General Assembly of the United Nations and accepted by a two-thirds majority of the States Parties to the present Protocol in accordance with their respective constitutional processes.

3. When amendments come into force, they shall be binding on those States Parties which have accepted them, other States Parties still being bound by the provisions of the present Protocol and any earlier amendment which they have accepted.

Article 12

1. Any State Party may denounce the present Protocol at any time by written notification addressed to

the Secretary-General of the United Nations. Denunciation shall take effect three months after the date of receipt of the notification by the Secretary-General.

2. Denunciation shall be without prejudice to the continued application of the provisions of the present Protocol to any communication submitted under article 2 before the effective date of denunciation.

Article 13

Irrespective of the notifications made under Article 8, paragraph 5, of the present Protocol, the Secretary-General of the United Nations shall inform all States referred to in article 48, paragraph 1, of the Covenant of the following particulars:

(a) Signatures, ratifications and accessions under article 8;

(b) The date of the entry into force of any amendments under article 11;

(c) Denunciations under article 12.

Article 14

1. The present Protocol, of which the Chinese, English, French, Russian and Spanish texts are equally authentic, shall be deposited in the archives of the United Nations.

2. The Secretary-General of the United Nations shall transmit certified copies of the present Protocol to all States referred to in article 48 of the Covenant.

APPENDIX I

EXCERPTS FROM THE
CHARTER OF THE
UNITED NATIONS

We the peoples of the United Nations determined

to save succeeding generations from the scourge of war, which twice in our lifetime has brought untold sorrow to mankind, and

to reaffirm faith in fundamental human rights, in the dignity and worth of the human person, in the equal rights of men and women and of nations large and small, and

to establish conditions under which justice and respect for the obligations arising from treaties and other sources of international law can be maintained, and

to promote social progress and better standards of life in larger freedom,

and for these ends

to practice tolerance and live together in peace with one another as good neighbors, and

to unite our strength to maintain international peace and security, and

to ensure, by the acceptance of principles and the institution of methods, that armed force shall not be used, save in the common interest, and

to employ international machinery for the promotion of the economic and social advancement of all peoples,

have resolved to combine our efforts
to accomplish these aims.

Accordingly, our respective Governments, through representatives assembled in the city of San Francisco, who have exhibited their full powers found to be in good and due form, have agreed to the present Charter of the United Nations and do hereby establish an international organization to be known as the United Nations.

◆ *Article 1*

The Purposes of the United Nations are:

1. To maintain international peace and security . . .

2. To develop friendly relations among nations based on respect for the principle of equal rights and self-determination of peoples, and to take other appropriate measures to strengthen universal peace;

3. To achieve international cooperation in solving international problems of an economic, social, cultural, or humanitarian character, and in promoting and encouraging respect for human rights and for fundamental freedoms for all without distinction as to race, sex, language, or religion; and

4. To be a center for harmonizing the actions of nations in the attainment of these common ends.

. . .

◆ *Article 13*

1. The General Assembly shall initiate studies and make recommendations for the purpose of:

. . .

b. promoting international cooperation in the economic, social, cultural, educational, and health fields, and assisting in the realization of human rights and fundamental freedoms for all without distinction as to race, sex, language, or religion.

. . .

◆ *Article 55*

With a view to the creation of conditions of stability and well-being which are necessary for peaceful and friendly relations among nations based on respect for the principle of equal rights and self-determination of peoples, the United Nations shall promote:

a. higher standards of living, full employment, and conditions of economic and social progress and development;

b. solutions of international economic, social, health, and related problems; and international cultural and educational cooperation; and

c. universal respect for, and observance of, human rights and fundamental freedoms for all without distinction as to race, sex, language or religion.

♦ *Article 56*

All Members pledge themselves to take joint and separate action in cooperation with the Organization for the achievement of the purposes set forth in Article 55.

. . .

♦ *Article 62*

1. The Economic and Social Council may . . .

2. . . . make recommendations for the purpose of promoting respect for, and observance of, human rights and fundamental freedoms for all.

3. It may prepare draft conventions for submission to the General Assembly, with respect to matters falling within its competence.

. . .

♦ *Article 68*

The Economic and Social Council shall set up commissions in economic and social fields and for the promotion of human rights, and such other commissions as may be required for the performance of its functions.

. . .

APPENDIX II

EXCERPTS FROM THE EUROPEAN CONVENTION FOR THE PROTECTION OF HUMAN RIGHTS AND FUNDAMENTAL FREEDOMS

The Governments signatory hereto, being Members of the Council of Europe,

Considering the Universal Declaration of Human Rights proclaimed by the General Assembly of the United Nations on 10th December 1948;

Considering that this Declaration aims at securing the universal and effective recognition and observance of the Rights therein declared;

Considering that the aim of the Council of Europe is the achievement of greater unity between its Members and that one of the methods by which that aim is to be pursued is the maintenance and further realization of Human Rights and Fundamental Freedoms;

Reaffirming their profound belief in those Fundamental Freedoms which are the foundation of justice and peace in the world and are best maintained on the one hand by an effective political democracy and on the other by a common understanding and observance of the Human Rights upon which they depend;

Being resolved, as the Governments of European countries which are likeminded and have a common heritage of political traditions, ideals, freedom and the rule of law to take the first steps for the collective enforcement of certain of the Rights stated in the Universal Declaration,

Have agreed as follows:

♦ *Article 1*

The High Contracting Parties shall secure to everyone within their jurisdiction the rights and freedoms defined in Section I of this Convention.

SECTION I

♦ *Article 2*

1. Everyone's right to life shall be protected by law. No one shall be deprived of his life intentionally save in the execution of a sentence of a court following his conviction of a crime for which this penalty is provided by law.

2. Deprivation of life shall not be regarded as inflicted in contravention of this Article when it results from the use of force which is no more than absolutely necessary:

(a) in defense of any person from unlawful violence;

(b) in order to effect a lawful arrest or to prevent the escape of a person lawfully detained;

(c) in action lawfully taken for the purpose of quelling a riot or insurrection.

♦ *Article 3*

No one shall be subjected to torture or to inhuman or degrading treatment or punishment.

♦ *Article 4*

1. No one shall be held in slavery or servitude.

2. No one shall be required to perform forced or compulsory labour.

3. For the purpose of this Article the term 'forced or compulsory labour' shall not include:

(a) any work required to be done in the ordinary course of detention imposed according to the provisions of Article 5 of this Convention or during conditional release from such detention;

(b) any service of a military character or, in case of conscientious objectors in countries where they are recognized, service exacted instead of compulsory military service;

(c) any service exacted in case of an emergency or calamity threatening the life or well-being of the community;

(d) any work or service which forms part of normal civic obligations.

♦ *Article 5*

1. Everyone has the right to liberty and security of person.

No one shall be deprived of his liberty save in the following cases and in accordance with a procedure prescribed by law:

(a) The lawful detention of a person after conviction by a competent court;

(b) the lawful arrest or detention of a person for non-compliance with the lawful order of a court or in order to secure the fulfilment of any obligations prescribed by law;

(c) the lawful arrest or detention of a person effected for the purpose of bringing him before the competent legal authority on reasonable suspicion of having committed an offence or when it is reasonably considered necessary to prevent his committing an offence or fleeing after having done so;

(d) the detention of a minor by lawful order for the purpose of educational supervision or his lawful detention for the purpose of bringing him before the competent legal authority;

(e) the lawful detention of persons for the prevention of the spreading of infectious diseases, of persons of unsound mind, alcoholics or drug addicts or vagrants;

(f) the lawful arrest or detention of a person to prevent his effecting an unauthorized entry into the country or of a person against whom action is being taken with a view to deportation or extradition.

2. Everyone who is arrested shall be informed promptly, in a language which he understands, of the reasons for his arrest and of any charge against him.

3. Everyone arrested or detained in accordance with the provisions of paragraph 1 *(c)* of this Article shall be brought promptly before a judge or other officer authorized by law to exercise judicial power and shall be entitled to trial within a reasonable time or to release pending trial. Release may be conditioned by guarantees to appear for trial.

4. Everyone who is deprived of his liberty by arrest or detention shall be entitled to take proceedings by which the lawfulness of his detention shall be decided speedily by a court and his release ordered if the detention is not lawful.

5. Everyone who has been the victim of arrest or detention in contravention of the provisions of this Article shall have an enforceable right to compensation.

♦ *Article 6*

1. In the determination of his civil rights and obligations or of any criminal charge against him, everyone is entitled to a fair and public hearing within a reasonable time by an independent and impartial tribunal established by law. Judgment shall be pronounced publicly but the press and public may be excluded from all or part of the trial in the interests of morals, public order or national security in a democratic society, where the interests of juveniles or the protection of the private life of the parties so require, or to the extent strictly necessary in the opinion of the court in special circumstances where publicity would prejudice the interests of justice.

2. Everyone charged with a criminal offence shall be presumed innocent until proved guilty according to law.

3. Everyone charged with a criminal offence has the following minimum rights:

(a) to be informed promptly, in a language which he understands and in detail, of the nature and cause of the accusation against him;

(b) to have adequate time and facilities for the preparation of his defence;

(c) to defend himself in person or through legal assistance of his own choosing or, if he has not sufficient means to pay for legal assistance, to be given it free when the interests of justice so require;

(d) to examine or have examined witnesses against him and to obtain the attendance and examination of witnesses on his behalf under the same conditions as witnesses against him;

(e) to have the free assistance of an interpreter if he cannot understand or speak the language used in court.

♦ *Article 7*

1. No one shall be held guilty of any criminal offence on account of any act or omission which did not constitute a criminal offence under national or international law at the time when it was committed. Nor shall a heavier penalty be imposed than the one that was applicable at the time the criminal offence was committed.

2. This Article shall not prejudice the trial and punishment of any person for any act or omission which, at the time when it was committed, was criminal according to the general principles of law recognized by civilized nations.

♦ *Article 8*

1. Everyone has the right to respect for his private and family life, his home and his correspondence.

2. There shall be no interference by a public authority with the exercise of this right except such as is in

accordance with the law and is necessary in a democratic society in the interests of national security, public safety or the economic well-being of the country, for the prevention of disorder or crime, for the protection of health or morals, or for the protection of the rights and freedoms of others.

♦ *Article 9*

1. Everyone has the right to freedom of thought, conscience and religion; this right includes freedom to change his religion or belief and freedom, either alone or in community with others and in public or private, to manifest his religion or belief, in worship, teaching, practice and observance.

2. Freedom to manifest one's religion or beliefs shall be subject only to such limitations as are prescribed by law and are necessary in a democratic society in the interests of public safety, for the protection of public order, health or morals, or for the protection of the rights and freedoms of others.

♦ *Article 10*

1. Everyone has the right to freedom of expression. This right shall include freedom to hold opinions and to receive and impart information and ideas without interference by public authority and regardless of frontiers. This Article shall not prevent States from requiring the licensing of broadcasting, television or cinema enterprises.

2. The exercise of these freedoms, since it carries with it duties and responsibilities, may be subject to such formalities, conditions, restrictions or penalties as are prescribed by law and are necessary in a democratic society, in the interests of national security, territorial integrity or public safety, for the prevention of disorder or crime, for the protection of health or morals, for the protection of the reputation or rights of others, for

preventing the disclosure of information received in confidence, or for maintaining the authority and impartiality of the judiciary.

♦ *Article 11*

1. Everyone has the right to freedom of peaceful assembly and to freedom of association with others, including the right to form and to join trade unions for the protection of his interests.

2. No restrictions shall be placed on the exercise of these rights other than such as are prescribed by law and are necessary in a democratic society in the interests of national security or public safety, for the prevention of disorder or crime, for the protection of health or morals or for the protection of the rights and freedoms of others. This Article shall not prevent the imposition of lawful restrictions on the exercise of these rights by members of the armed forces, of the police or of the administration of the State.

♦ *Article 12*

Men and women of marriageable age have the right to marry and to found a family, according to the national laws governing the exercise of this right.

♦ *Article 13*

Everyone whose rights and freedoms as set forth in this Convention are violated shall have an effective remedy before a national authority notwithstanding that the violation has been committed by persons acting in an official capacity.

♦ *Article 14*

The enjoyment of the rights and freedoms set forth in this Convention shall be secured without discrimination on any ground such as sex, race, colour, language, religion, political or other opinion, national or social origin, association with a national minority, property, birth or other status.

♦ *Article 15*

1. In time of war or other public emergency threatening the life of the nation any High Contracting Party may take measures derogating from its obligations under this Convention to the extent strictly required by the exigencies of the situation, provided that such measures are not inconsistent with its other obligations under international law.

2. No derogation from Article 2, except in respect of deaths resulting from lawful acts of war, or from Articles 3, 4 (paragraph 1) and 7 shall be made under this provision.

3. Any High Contracting Party availing itself of this right of derogation shall keep the Secretary-General of the Council of Europe fully informed of the measures which it has taken and the reasons therefor. It shall also inform the Secretary General of the Council of Europe when such measures have ceased to operate and the provisions of the Convention are again being fully executed.

♦ *Article 16*

Nothing in Articles 10, 11 and 14 shall be regarded as preventing the High Contracting Parties from imposing restrictions on the political activity of aliens.

♦ *Article 17*

Nothing in this Convention may be interpreted as implying for any State, group or person any right to engage in any activity or perform any act aimed at the destruction of any of the rights and freedoms set forth herein or at their limitation to a greater extent than is provided for in the Convention.

♦ *Article 18*

The restrictions permitted under this Convention to

the said rights and freedoms shall not be applied for any purpose other than those for which they have been prescribed.

. . .

FIRST PROTOCOL

The Governments signatory hereto, being Members of the Council of Europe,

Being resolved to take steps to ensure the collective enforcement of certain rights and freedoms other than those already included in Section 1 of the Convention for the Protection of Human Rights and Fundamental Freedoms signed at Rome on 4th November, 1950 (hereinafter referred to as 'the Convention'),

Have agreed as follows:

♦ *Article 1*

Every natural or legal person is entitled to the peaceful enjoyment of his possessions. No one shall be deprived of his possessions except in the public interest and subject to the conditions provided for by law and by the general principles of international law.

The preceding provisions shall not, however, in any way impair the right of a State to enforce such laws as it deems necessary to control the use of property in accordance with the general interest or to secure the payment of taxes or other contributions or penalties.

♦ *Article 2*

No person shall be denied the right to education. In the exercise of any functions which it assumes in relation to education and to teaching, the State shall respect the right of parents to ensure such education and teaching in conformity with their own religious and philosophical convictions.

♦ *Article 3*

The High Contracting Parties undertake to hold free elections at reasonable intervals by secret ballot, under conditions which will ensure the free expression of the opinion of the people in the choice of the legislature.
. . .

FOURTH PROTOCOL
SECURING CERTAIN RIGHTS AND FREEDOMS OTHER THAN THOSE ALREADY INCLUDED IN THE CONVENTION AND IN THE FIRST PROTOCOL THERETO

The Governments signatory hereto, being Members of the Council of Europe,

Being resolved to take steps to ensure the collective enforcement of certain rights and freedoms other than those already included in Section 1 of the Convention for the Protection of Human Rights and Fundamental Freedoms signed at Rome on 4th November 1950 (hereinafter referred to as 'the Convention') and in Articles 1 to 3 of the First Protocol to the Convention, signed at Paris on 20th March 1952,

Have agreed as follows:

♦ *Article 1*

No one shall be deprived of his liberty merely on the ground of inability to fulfil a contractual obligation.

♦ *Article 2*

1. Everyone lawfully within that territory of a State shall, within that territory, have the right to liberty of movement and freedom to choose his residence.

2. Everyone shall be free to leave any country, including his own.

3. No restrictions shall be placed on the exercise of these rights other than such as are in accordance with

law and are necessary in a democratic society in the interests of national security or public safety, for the maintenance of *ordre public,* for the prevention of crime, for the protection of health or morals, or for the protection of the rights and freedoms of others.

4. The rights set forth in paragraph 1 may also be subject, in particular areas, to restrictions imposed in accordance with law and justified by the public interest in a democratic society.

♦ *Article 3*

1. No one shall be expelled, by means either of an individual or of a collective measure, from the territory of the State of which he is a national.

2. No one shall be deprived of the right to enter the territory of the State of which he is a national.

♦ *Article 4*

Collective expulsion of aliens is prohibited.

. . .

EXCERPTS FROM THE AMERICAN CONVENTION ON HUMAN RIGHTS

PREAMBLE

The American States signatory to the present Convention,
Reaffirming *their intention to consolidate in this hemisphere, within the framework of democratic institutions, a system of personal liberty and social justice based on respect for the essential rights of man;*

Recognizing *that the essential rights of man are not derived from one's being a national of a certain State, but are based upon attributes of the human personality, and that they therefore justify international protection in the form of a convention reinforcing or complementing the protection provided by the domestic law of the American States;*

Considering *that these principles have been set forth in the Charter of the Organization of American States, in the American Declaration of the Rights and Duties of Man, and in the Universal Declaration of Human Rights, and that they have been reaffirmed and refined in other international instruments, worldwide as well as regional in scope;*

Reiterating *that, in accordance with the Universal Declaration of Human Rights, the ideal of free men enjoying freedom from fear and want can be achieved only if conditions are created whereby everyone may enjoy his economic, social and cultural rights, as well as his civil and political rights; and*

Considering *that the Third Special Inter-American Conference (Buenos Aires, 1967) approved the incorporation into the Charter of the Organization itself of broader standards with respect to economic, social and educational rights and resolved that an inter-American convention on human rights should determine the structure, competence, and procedure of the organs responsible for these matters,*

Have agreed upon the following:

PART I.
STATE OBLIGATIONS AND
RIGHTS PROTECTED

CHAPTER I.
GENERAL OBLIGATIONS

♦ *Article 1. Obligation to Respect Rights*

1. The States Parties to this Convention undertake to respect the rights and freedoms recognized herein and to ensure to all persons subject to their jurisdiction the free and full exercise of those rights and freedoms, without any discrimination for reasons of race, color, sex, language, religion, political or other opinion, national or social origin, economic status, birth, or any other social condition.

2. For the purposes of this Convention, 'person' means every human being.

♦ *Article 2. Domestic Legal Effects*

Where the exercise of any of the rights or freedoms referred to in Article 1 is not already ensured by legislative or other provisions, the States Parties undertake to adopt, in accordance with their constitutional processes and the provisions of this Convention, such legislative or other measures as may be necessary to give effect to those rights or freedoms.

CHAPTER II.
CIVIL AND POLITICAL RIGHTS

♦ *Article 3. Right to Juridical Personality*

Every person has the right to recognition as a person before the law.

♦ *Article 4. Right to Life*

1. Every person has the right to have his life respected. This right shall be protected by law, and, in general, from the moment of conception. No one shall be arbitrarily deprived of his life.

2. In countries that have not abolished the death penalty, this may be imposed only for the most serious crimes and pursuant to a final judgment rendered by a competent court and in accordance with a law establishing such punishment, enacted prior to the commission of the crime. Its application shall not be extended to crimes to which it does not presently apply.

3. The death penalty shall not be re-established in States that have abolished it.

4. In no case shall capital punishment be inflicted for political offences or related common crimes.

5. Capital punishment shall not be imposed upon persons who, at the time the crime was committed, were under eighteen years of age or over seventy years of age; nor shall it be applied to pregnant women.

6. Every person condemned to death shall have the right to apply for amnesty, pardon, or commutation of sentence, which may be granted in all cases. Capital punishment shall not be imposed while such a petition is pending a decision by the competent authority.

♦ *Article 5. Freedom from Torture*

1. Every person has the right to have his physical, mental, and moral integrity respected.

2. No one shall be subjected to torture or to cruel,

inhuman, or degrading punishment or treatment. All persons deprived of their liberty shall be treated with respect for the inherent dignity of the human person.

3. Punishment shall not be extended to any person other than the criminal.

4. Accused persons shall, save in exceptional circumstances, be segregated from convicted persons, and shall be subject to separate treatment appropriate to their status as unconvicted persons.

5. Minors while subject to criminal proceedings shall be separated from adults and brought before specialized tribunals, as speedily as possible, so that they may be treated in accordance with their status as minors.

6. Punishments consisting of deprivation of liberty shall have as an essential aim the reform and social readaptation of the prisoners.

◆ *Article 6. Freedom from Slavery*

1. No one shall be subject to slavery or to involuntary servitude which are prohibited in all their forms, as are the slave trade and traffic in women.

2. No one shall be required to perform forced or compulsory labour. This provision shall not be interpreted to mean that, in those countries in which the penalty established for certain crimes is deprivation of liberty at forced labour, the carrying out of such a sentence imposed by a competent court is prohibited. Forced labour shall not adversely affect the dignity or the physical or intellectual capacity of the prisoner.

3. For the purpose of this article the following do not constitute forced or compulsory labour:

(a) any work or service normally required of a person imprisoned in execution of a sentence or formal decision passed by the competent judicial authority. Such work or service shall be carried out under the supervision and control of public authorities, and any persons performing such work or service shall not be

placed at the disposal of any private party, company, or juridical person;

(b) any military service and, in countries in which conscientious objectors are recognized, any national service that the law may provide for in lieu of that service;

(c) any service exacted in time of danger or calamity that threatens the existence or the well-being of the community; or

(d) any work or service that forms part of normal civic obligations.

◆ *Article 7. Right to Personal Liberty*

1. Every person has the right to personal liberty and security.

2. No one shall be deprived of his physical liberty except for the reasons and under the conditions established beforehand by the Constitution of the State Party concerned or a law established pursuant thereto.

3. No one shall be subject to arbitrary arrest or imprisonment.

4. Anyone who is detained shall be informed of the reasons for his detention and shall be promptly notified of the charge or charges against him.

5. Any person detained shall be brought promptly before a judge or other officer authorized by law to exercise judicial power and shall be entitled to trial within a reasonable time or to be released without prejudice to continuation of the proceedings. His release may be subject to guarantees to assure his appearance at trial.

6. Anyone who is deprived of his liberty shall be entitled to recourse to a competent court, in order that the court may decide without delay on the lawfulness of his arrest or detention and order his release if the arrest or detention is unlawful. In States Parties whose laws provide that anyone who believes himself to be threatened with deprivation of his liberty is entitled to recourse to a

competent court in order that it may decide on the lawfulness of such threat, this remedy may not be restricted or abolished. The interested party or another person in his behalf is entitled to seek these remedies.

7. No one shall be detained for debt. This principle shall not limit the orders of a competent judicial authority issued for nonfulfillment of duties of support.

♦ *Article 8. Right to a Fair Trial*

1. Every person shall have the right to a hearing with due guarantees and within a reasonable time, by a competent, independent and impartial tribunal, previously established by law, in the substantiation of any accusation of a criminal nature made against him or for the determination of his rights or obligations of a civil, labour, fiscal, or any other nature.

2. Every person accused of a serious crime has the right to be presumed innocent so long as his guilt has not been proven according to law. During the proceedings, every person is entitled, with full equality, to the following minimum guarantees:

(a) the right of the accused to be assisted free by a translator or interpreter, if he does not understand or does not speak the language of the tribunal or court;

(b) prior notification in detail to the accused of the charges against him;

(c) adequate time and means for the preparation of his defense;

(d) the right of the accused to defend himself personally or to be assisted by legal counsel of his own choosing, and to communicate freely and privately with his counsel;

(e) the inalienable right to be assisted by counsel provided by the State, paid or not as the domestic law provides, if the accused does not defend himself personally or engage his own counsel within the time period established by law;

(f) the right of the defence to examine witnesses present in the court and to obtain the appearance, as witnesses, of experts or other persons who may throw light on the facts;

(g) the right not to be compelled to be a witness against himself or to plead guilty; and

(h) the right to appeal to a higher court.

3. A confession of guilt by the accused shall be valid only if it is made without coercion of any kind.

4. An accused person, acquitted by a non-appealable judgment, shall not be subjected to a new trial for the same cause.

5. Criminal procedure shall be public, except in so far as may be necessary to protect the interests of justice.

♦ *Article 9. Freedom from Ex Post Facto Laws*

No one shall be convicted of any act or omission that did not constitute a criminal offence, under the applicable law, at the time it was committed. A heavier penalty shall not be imposed than the one that was applicable at the time the criminal offence was committed. If subsequently to the commission of the offence the law provides for the imposition of a lighter punishment, the guilty person shall benefit therefrom.

♦ *Article 10. Right to Compensation*

Every person shall have the right to be compensated in accordance with the law in the event he has been sentenced by a final judgment through a miscarriage of justice.

♦ *Article 11. Right to Privacy*

1. Everyone has the right to have his honour respected and his dignity recognized.

2. No one may be the object of arbitrary or abusive interference with his private life, his family, his home, or his correspondence, or of unlawful attacks on his honour or reputation.

3. Everyone has a right to the protection of the law against such interference or attacks.

♦ *Article 12. Freedom of Conscience and Religion*

1. Everyone shall have the right to freedom of conscience and of religion. This right shall include freedom to maintain or to change his religion or beliefs, and freedom to profess or disseminate his religion or beliefs either individually or in community with others, in public or in private.

2. No one shall be subject to restriction that might impair his freedom to maintain or to change his religion or beliefs.

3. Freedom to manifest one's religion and beliefs may be subject only to the limitations prescribed by law that are necessary to protect public safety, order, health, or morals, or the rights or freedoms of others.

4. Parents or guardians, as the case may be, have the right to provide for religious and moral education of their children, or wards, that is in accord with their own convictions.

♦ *Article 13. Freedom of Thought and Expression*

1. Everyone shall have the right to freedom of thought and expression. This right shall include freedom to seek, receive, and impart information and ideas of all kinds, regardless of frontiers, either orally, in writing, in print, in the form of art, or through any other medium of his choice.

2. The exercise of the right provided for in the foregoing paragraph shall not be subject to prior censorship but shall be subject to subsequent liability, which shall be expressly established by law and be necessary in order to ensure:

(a) respect for the rights or reputations of others; or
(b) the protection of national security, public order, or public health or morals.

3. The right of expression may not be restricted by indirect methods or means, such as the abuse of government or private controls over newsprint, radio broadcasting frequencies, or implements or equipment used in the dissemination of information, or by any other means tending to impede the communication and circulation of ideas and opinions.

4. Notwithstanding the provisions of paragraph 2 above, public entertainments may be subject by law to prior censorship, for the sole purpose of regulating access to them for the moral protection of childhood and adolescence.

5. Any propaganda for war and any advocacy of national, racial or religious hatred that constitute incitements to lawless violence or any other similar illegal action against any person or group of persons on any grounds including those of race, colour, religion, language, or national origin shall be considered as offences punishable by law.

♦ *Article 14. Right of Reply*

1. Anyone injured by inaccurate or offensive statements or ideas disseminated to the public in general by a legally regulated medium of communication has the right to reply or make a correction using the same communications outlet, under such conditions as the law may establish.

2. The correction or reply shall not in any case remit other legal liabilities that may have been incurred.

3. For the effective protection of honour and reputation, every publication, and every newspaper, motion picture, radio, and television company, shall have a person responsible, who is not protected by immunities or special privileges.

♦ *Article 15. Right of Assembly*

The right of peaceful assembly, without arms, is

recognized. No restrictions may be placed on the exercise of this right other than those imposed in conformity with the law and necessary in a democratic society in the interests of national security or public safety or public order, or to protect public health or morals or the rights or freedoms of others.

♦ *Article 16. Freedom of Association*

1. Everyone shall have the right to associate freely for ideological, religious, political, economic, labour, social, cultural, sports, or other purposes.

2. Exercise of this right shall be subject only to such restrictions established by law as may be necessary in a democratic society, in the interest of national security, public safety, or public order, or to protect public health or morals or the rights and freedoms of others.

3. The provisions of this article do not bar the imposition of legal restrictions, including even deprivation of the exercise of the right of association, on members of the armed forces and the police.

♦ *Article 17. Rights of the Family*

1. The family is the natural and fundamental group unit of society and is entitled to protection by society and the State.

2. The right of men and women of marriageable age to marry and to raise a family shall be recognized, if they meet the conditions required by domestic laws, in so far as such conditions do not affect the principle of non-discrimination established in this Convention.

3. No marriage shall be entered into without the free and full consent of the intending spouses.

4. The States Parties shall take appropriate steps to ensure the equality of rights and the adequate balancing of responsibilities of the spouses as to marriage, during marriage, and in the event of its dissolution. In case of dissolution, provision shall be made for the necessary

protection of any children solely on the basis of their own best interests.

5. The law shall recognize equal rights for children born out of wedlock and those born in wedlock.

♦ *Article 18. Right to a Name*

Every person has the right to a given name and to the surnames of his parents or that of one of them. The law shall regulate the manner in which this right shall be ensured for all, by the use of assumed names if necessary.

♦ *Article 19. Rights of the Child*

Every minor child has the right to the measures of protection required by his condition as a minor, on the part of his family, society, and the State.

♦ *Article 20. Right to a Nationality*

1. Every person has the right to a nationality.

2. Every person has the right to the nationality of the State in whose territory he was born if he does not have the right to any other nationality.

3. No one shall be arbitrarily deprived of his nationality or of the right to change it.

♦ *Article 21. Right to Property*

1. Everyone has the right to the use and enjoyment of his property. The law may subordinate such use and enjoyment to the interest of society.

2. No one shall be deprived of his property except upon payment of just compensation, for reasons of public utility or social interest, and in the cases and according to the forms established by law.

3. Usury and any other form of exploitation of man by man shall be prohibited by law.

♦ *Article 22. Freedom of Movement and Residence*

1. Every person lawfully in the territory of a State

Party shall have the right to move about in it and to reside in it subject to the provisions of the law.

2. Every person shall have the right to leave any country freely, including his own.

3. The exercise of the foregoing rights may be restricted only pursuant to a law, to the extent indispensable in a democratic society in order to prevent crime or to protect national security, public safety, public order, public morals, public health, or the rights or freedoms of others.

4. The exercise of the rights recognized in paragraph 1 may also be restricted by law in designated zones for reasons of public interest.

5. No one may be expelled from the territory of the State of which he is a national or be deprived of the right to enter it.

6. An alien lawfully in the territory of a State Party to this Convention may be expelled from it only pursuant to a decision reached in accordance with law.

7. Every person shall have the right to seek and be granted asylum in a foreign territory, in accordance with the legislation of the State and international Conventions, in the event he is being pursued for political or related common crimes.

8. In no case may an alien be deported or returned to a country, regardless of whether or not it is his country of origin, if in that country his right to life or personal freedom is in danger of being violated because of his race, nationality, religion, social status, or political opinions.

9. The collective expulsion of aliens is prohibited.

♦ *Article 23. Right to Participate in Government*

1. Every citizen shall enjoy the following rights and opportunities:

(a) to take part in the conduct of public affairs,

directly or through freely chosen representatives;
(b) to vote and to be elected at genuine periodic elections, which shall be by universal and equal suffrage and by secret ballot that guarantees the free expression of the will of the voters; and

(c) to have access, under general conditions of equality, to the public service of his country.

2. The law may regulate the exercise of the rights and opportunities referred to in the preceding paragraph, exclusively on the basis of age, nationality, residence, language, education, civil and mental capacity, and conviction by a competent judge in criminal proceedings.

♦ *Article 24. Right to Equal Protection*

All persons are equal before the law. Consequently, they are entitled, without discrimination, to equal protection of the law.

♦ *Article 25. Right to Judicial Protection*

1. Everyone has the right to simple and prompt recourse, or any other effective recourse, to a competent court or tribunal, for protection against acts that violate his fundamental rights recognized by the Constitution or laws of a State or by this Convention, even though such violation may have been committed by persons acting in the course of their official duties.

2. The States Parties undertake:

(a) to ensure that any person claiming such remedy shall have his right thereto determined by the competent authority provided for by the legal system of the State;

(b) to develop the possibilities of judicial remedy; and

(c) to ensure that the competent authorities shall enforce such remedies when granted.

CHAPTER III.
ECONOMIC, SOCIAL AND CULTURAL RIGHTS

♦ *Article 26. Progressive Development*

The States Parties undertake to adopt measures, both internally and through international cooperation, especially with regard to economic and technical matters, with a view to achieving progressively, by legislation or other appropriate means, the full realization of the rights implicit in the economic, social, educational, scientific, and cultural standards set forth in the Charter of the Organization of American States as amended by the Protocol of Buenos Aires.

CHAPTER IV.
SUSPENSION OF GUARANTEES,
INTERPRETATION, AND APPLICATION

♦ *Article 27. Suspension of Guarantees*

1. In time of war, public danger, or other emergency that threatens the independence or security of a State Party, it may take measures derogating from its obligations under the present Convention to the extent and for the period of time strictly required by the exigencies of the situation, provided that such measures are not inconsistent with its other obligations under international law and do not involve discrimination on the ground of race, colour, sex, language, religion, or social origin.

2. The foregoing provision does not authorize any suspension of the following articles: Article 3 (Right to juridical personality); Article 4 (Right to life); Article 5 (Freedom from torture); Article 6 (Freedom from slavery); Article 9 (Freedom from *post facto* laws); Article 12 (Freedom of conscience and religion); Article 17 (Rights of the family); Article 18 (Right to a name); Article 19 (Rights of the child); Article 20 (Right to

nationality); and Article 23 (Right to participate in government), or of the judicial guarantees essential for the protection of such rights.

3. Any State Party availing itself of the rights of suspension shall immediately inform the other States Parties, through the Secretary-General of the Organization of American States, of the provisions the application of which it has suspended, the reasons that gave rise to the suspension, and the date set for the termination of such suspension.

♦ *Article 28. Federal Clause*

Where a State Party is constituted as a federal State, the national government of such State Party shall implement all the provisions of the Convention over whose subject matter it exercises legislative and judicial jurisdiction.

With respect to the provision over whose subject matter the constituent units of the federal State have jurisdiction, the national government shall immediately take suitable measures, in accordance with its Constitution and its laws, to the end that the competent authorities of the constituent units may adopt appropriate provisions to comply with this Convention.

Whenever two or more States Parties agree to form a federation or other type of association they shall take care that the resulting federal or other compact contains the provisions necessary for continuing and rendering effective the standards of this Convention in the new State that is organized.

♦ *Article 29. Restrictions Regarding Interpretation*

No provision of this Convention shall be interpreted as:
(a) permitting any State Party, group, or person to suppress the enjoyment or exercise of the rights and freedoms recognized in this Convention or to restrict them to a greater extent than is provided herein;
(b) restricting the enjoyment or exercise of any right

or freedom recognized by virtue of the laws of any State Party or by virtue of another Convention to which one of the said States is a Party;

(c) precluding other rights or guarantees that are inherent in the human personality or derived from representative democracy as a form of government; or

(d) excluding or limiting the effect that the American Declaration of the Rights and Duties of Man and other international Acts of the same nature may have.

♦ *Article 30. Scope of Restrictions*

The restrictions that, pursuant to this Convention, may be placed on the enjoyment or exercise of the rights or freedoms recognized herein may not be applied except in accordance with laws enacted for reasons of general interest and for the purpose of which the restrictions have been established.

♦ *Article 31. Recognition of Other Rights*

Other rights and freedoms recognized by virtue of the procedures established in Articles 76 and 77 may be included in the system of protection of this Convention.

CHAPTER V.
PERSONAL RESPONSIBILITIES

♦ *Article 32. Relationships Between Duties and Rights*

1. Every person has responsibilities to his family, his community, and mankind.

2. The rights of each person are limited by the rights of others, by the security of all, and by the just demands of the general welfare, in a democratic society.

. . .

APPENDIX IV
EXCERPTS FROM THE HELSINKI ACCORD

A. DECLARATION ON PRINCIPLES GUIDING RELATIONS BETWEEN PARTICIPATING STATES

VII. Respect for human rights and fundamental freedoms, including the freedom of thought, conscience, religion or belief

The participating States will respect human rights and fundamental freedoms, including the freedom of thought, conscience, religion or belief, for all without distinction as to race, sex, language or religion.

They will promote and encourage the effective exercise of civil, political, economic, social, cultural and other rights and freedoms all of which derive from the inherent dignity of the human person and are essential for his free and full development.

Within this framework the participating States will recognize and respect the freedom of the individual to profess and practice, alone or in community with others, religion or belief acting in accordance with the dictates of his own conscience.

The participating States on whose territory national minorities exist will respect the right of persons belonging to such minorities to equality before the law, will afford them the full opportunity for the actual enjoyment of human rights and fundamental freedoms and will, in this manner, protect their legitimate interests in this sphere.

The participating States recognize the universal significance of human rights and fundamental freedoms, respect for which is an essential factor for the peace, justice and well-being necessary to ensure the development of friendly relations and co-operation among themselves as among all States.

They will constantly respect these rights and freedoms in their mutual relations and will endeavour jointly and separately, including in co-operation with the United Nations, to promote universal and effective respect for them.

They confirm the right of the individual to know and act upon his rights and duties in this field.

In the field of human rights and fundamental freedoms, the participating States will act in conformity with the purposes and principles of the Charter of the United Nations and with the Universal Declaration of Human Rights. They will also fulfill their obligations as set forth in the international declarations and agreements in this field, including inter alia the International Covenants on Human Rights, by which they may be bound.

VIII. *Equal rights and self-determination of peoples*

The participating States will respect the equal rights of peoples and their right to self-determination, acting at all times in conformity with the purposes and principles of the Charter of the United Nations and with the relevant norms of international law, including those relating to territorial integrity of States.

By virtue of the principle of equal rights and self-determination of peoples, all peoples always have the right, in full freedom, to determine, when and as they wish, their internal and external political status, without external interference, and to pursue as they wish their political, economic, social and cultural development.

The participating States reaffirm the universal significance of respect for an effective exercise of equal rights and self-determination of peoples for the development of friendly relations among themselves or among all States; they also recall the importance of the elimination of any form of violation of this principle.

B. MATTERS RELATED TO GIVING EFFECT TO CERTAIN OF THE ABOVE PRINCIPLES

1. Human Contacts

The participating States,

Considering the development of contacts to be an important element in the strengthening of friendly relations and trust among peoples,

Affirming, in relation to their present effort to improve conditions in this area, the importance they attach to humanitarian considerations,

Desiring in this spirit to develop, with the continuance of détente, further efforts to achieve continuing progress in this field

And conscious that the questions relevant hereto must be settled by the States concerned under mutually acceptable conditions,

Make it their aim to facilitate freer movement and contacts, individually and collectively, whether privately or officially, among persons, institutions and organizations of the participating States, and to contribute to the solution of the humanitarian problems that arise in that connexion,

Declare their readiness to these ends to take measures which they consider appropriate and to conclude agreements or arrangements among themselves, as may be needed, and

Express their intention now to proceed to the implementation of the following:

(a) Contacts and Regular Meetings on the Basis of Family Ties

In order to promote further development of contacts on the basis of family ties the participating States will favourably consider applications for travel with the purpose of allowing persons to enter or leave their territory temporarily, and on a regular basis if desired, in order to visit members of their families.

Applications for temporary visits to meet members of their families will be dealt with without distinction as to the country of origin or destination: existing requirements for travel documents and visas will be applied in this spirit. The preparation and issue of such documents and visas will be effected within reasonable time limits: cases of urgent necessity—such as serious illness or death —will be given priority treatment. They will take such steps as may be necessary to ensure that the fees for official travel documents and visas are acceptable.

They confirm that the presentation of an application concerning contacts on the basis of family ties will not modify the rights and obligations of the applicant or of members of his family.

(b) Reunification of Families

The participating States will deal in a positive and humanitarian spirit with the applications of persons who wish to be reunited with members of their family, with special attention being given to requests of an urgent character—such as requests submitted by persons who are ill or old.

They will deal with applications in this field as expeditiously as possible.

They will lower where necessary the fees charged in connexion with these applications to ensure that they are at a moderate level.

Applications for the purpose of family reunification which are not granted may be renewed at the appropriate level and will be reconsidered at reasonably short intervals by the authorities of the country of residence or destination, whichever is concerned; under such circumstances fees will be charged only when applications are granted.

Persons whose applications for family reunification are granted may bring with them or ship their household and personal effects; to this end the participating States will use all possibilities provided by existing regulations.

Until members of the same family are reunited meetings and contacts between them may take place in accordance with the modalities for contacts on the basis of family ties.

The participating States will support the efforts of Red Cross and Red Crescent Societies concerned with the problems of family reunification.

They confirm that the presentation of an application concerning family reunification will not modify the rights and obligations of the applicant or of members of his family.

The receiving participating State will take appropriate care with regard to employment for persons from other participating States who take up permanent residence in that State in connexion with family reunification with its citizens and see that they are afforded opportunities equal to those enjoyed by its own citizens for education, medical assistance and social security.

(c) Marriage between Citizens of Different States

The participating States will examine favourably and on the basis of humanitarian considerations requests for exit or entry permits from persons who have decided to marry a citizen from another participating State.

The processing and issuing of the documents required for the above purposes and for the marriage will be in accordance with the provisions accepted for family reunification.

In dealing with requests from couples from different participating States, once married, to enable them and the minor children of their marriage to transfer their permanent residence to a State in which either one is normally a resident, the participating States will also apply the provisions accepted for family reunification.

(d) Travel for Personal or Professional Reasons

The participating States intend to facilitate wider travel by their citizens for personal or professional reasons and to this end they intend in particular:

—gradually to simplify and to administer flexibly the procedures for exit and entry;

—to ease regulations concerning movement of citizens from the other participating States in their territory, with due regard to security requirements.

They will endeavour gradually to lower, where necessary, the fees for visas and official travel documents.

They intend to consider, as necessary, means—including, in so far as appropriate, the conclusion of multilateral or bilateral consular conventions or other relevant agreements or understandings—for the improvement of arrangements to provide consular services, including legal and consular assistance.

*   *   *

They confirm that religious faiths, institutions and organizations, practicing within the constitutional framework of the participating States, and their representatives can, in the field of their activities, have contacts and meetings among themselves and exchange information.

. . .

APPENDIX V
SIGNATURES AND RATIFICATIONS

What follows is a list of all countries that have signed or ratified the two Covenants or who are parties to the American Convention, the European Convention, or the Helsinki Accord, as of January 1981. Note that a country such as the United States that has signed the Covenants but not ratified them has not yet committed itself to be bound by them under international law. The Universal Declaration, on the other hand, does not require ratification but has been implicitly or explicitly accepted by all nations belonging to the United Nations.

Key:

C1S = signed the Covenant on Economic, Social and Cultural Rights

C2S = signed the Covenant on Civil and Political Rights

C1R = (signed and) ratified (or acceded to) the Covenant on Economic, Social and Cultural Rights

C2R = (signed and) ratified (or acceded to) the Covenant on Civil and Political Rights

OPS = signed the Optional Protocol to the Covenant on Civil and Political Rights

OPR = (signed and) ratified (or acceded to) the Optional Protocol to the Covenant on Civil and Political Rights

a41 = ratified Article 41 of the Covenant on Civil and Political Rights

ES = signed the European Convention on Human Rights

ER = (signed and) ratified (or acceded to) the European Convention on Human Rights

ER(exc 4) = ratified the European Convention except for the Fourth Protocol

AS = signed the American Convention on Human Rights

AR = (signed and) ratified (or acceded to) the American Convention on Human Rights

H = parties to the Helsinki Accord

Algeria C1S, C2S
Argentina C1S, C2S
Australia C1R, C2R
Austria C1R, C2R, OPS, a41, ER, H
Barbados C1R, C2R, OPR, AS
Belgium C1S, C2S, ER, H
Bolivia AR
Bulgaria C1R, C2R, H
Byelorussian SSR C1R, C2R
Canada C1R, C2R, OPR, a41, H
Chile C1R, C2R, AS
Colombia C1R, C2R, OPR, AR
Costa Rica C1R, C2R, OPR, AR
Cyprus C1R, C2R, OPS, ER, H
Czechoslovakia C1R, C2R, H
Democratic Kampuchea C1S, C2S
Denmark C1R, C2R, OPR, a41, ER, H
Dominican Republic C1R, C2R, OPR, AR
Ecuador C1R, C2R, OPR, AR
Egypt C1S, C2S
El Salvador C1R, C2R, OPS, AR
Finland C1R, C2R, OPR, a41, H
France C1R, ER, H
Gambia C1R, C2R
German Democratic Republic (East Germany) C1R, C2R, H

Germany, Federal Republic of (West Germany) C1R, C2R, a41, ER, H
Greece ER, H
Grenada AR
Guatemala AR
Guinea C1R, C2R, OPS
Guyana C1R, C2R
Haiti AR
Holy See H
Honduras C1S, C2S, OPS, AR
Hungary C1R, C2R, H
Iceland C1R, C2R, OPR, ER, H
India C1R, C2R
Iran C1R, C2R
Iraq C1R, C2R
Ireland C1S, C2S, ER, H
Israel C1S, C2S
Italy C1R, C2R, OPR, a41, ER(exc 4), H
Jamaica C1R, C2R, OPR, AR
Japan C1R, C2R
Jordan C1R, C2R
Kenya C1R, C2R
Lebanon C1R, C2R
Liberia C1S, C2S
Libyan Arab Republic, C1R, C2R
Liechtenstein ES, H
Luxembourg C1S, C2S, ER, H
Madagascar C1R, C2R, OPR
Mali C1R, C2R
Malta C1S, ER, H
Mauritius C1R, C2R, OPR

Mexico AR
Monaco H
Mongolia C1R, C2R
Morocco C1R, C2R
Netherlands C1R, C2R, OPR, ER, H
New Zealand C1R, C2R, a41
Nicaragua C1R, C2R, OPR, AR
Norway C1R, C2R, OPR, a41, ER, H.
Panama C1R, C2R, OPR, AR
Paraguay AS
Peru C1R, C2R, OPR, AR
Philippines C1R, C2S, OPS
Poland C1R, C2R, H
Portugal C1R, C2R, OPS, ER, H
Romania C1R, C2R, H
Rwanda C1R, C2R
San Marino H
Senegal C1R, C2R, OPR, a41
Spain C1R, C2R, ES, H
Sri Lanka C1R, C2R, a41
Suriname C1R, C2R, OPR

Sweden C1R, C2R, OPR, a41, ER, H
Switzerland ER, H
Syrian Arab Republic C1R, C2R
Taiwan C1S, C2S
Trinidad and Tobago C1R, C2R
Tunisia C1R, C2R
Turkey ER, H
Ukrainian SSR C1R, C2R
Union of Soviet Socialist Republics C1R, C2R, H
United Kingdom C1R, C2R, a41, ER(exc 4), H
United Republic of Tanzania C1R, C2R
United States of America C1S, C2S, AS, H
Uruguay C1R, C2R, OPR, AS
Venezuela C1R, C2R, OPR, AR
Yugoslavia C1R, C2R, H
Zaire C1R, C2R, OPR

AFTERWORD

by Adolfo Pérez Esquivel

The struggle towards the greater humanization of man—to move, as Pope Paul VI said, from conditions less humane towards those that are more humane—is perhaps the history of humankind. And today the defense of human rights is a special part of this process.

The last few decades have seen a more extended and internationalized conscience in respect to human rights, such that we are confronted with and increasingly forced toward a deeper understanding of what the struggle for human rights means.

The International Bill of Human Rights of the United Nations, along with the various laws, conventions, and accords agreed to by diverse international organizations, is a sign of the progressive capturing of the general conscience of humanity by the issues of the rights of man and the rights of peoples.

This however is not enough to bring about the full desired effect; the invasion of these same rights continues on a daily basis. Parallel to this growing sense of conscience we find an unchanging quantity of violations of individual and collective rights. Frequently in speaking of human rights reference is made to special, tragic circumstances such as murders, disappearances, tortures, imprisonments, etc. Firm condemnations of these violations are only a part of the struggle, speaking to the most visible and distressing aspect of the situation. But it is also necessary to establish a more global perspective on the problem, in order to explore the *causes* of the violation of human rights and of the rights of peoples.

The struggle in defense of these rights cannot limit its perspective and its actions to the confrontation between the individual and the state. Not only must the rights of individuals be repossessed for the sake of personal liberty, but so also must collective rights, the rights of peoples, be reclaimed on behalf of the social unit. Therefore the point is not simply to oppose the individual to the state, but also to go deeply into the structural causes, the systems of injustice that generate oppressive forms that violate human rights.

We must establish the struggle for human rights as part of the struggle for the rights of peoples, distinguishing social structures that generate violations of these rights from those that can contribute to deliverance from all types of domination, that can contribute to the development of justice and peace and to respect for the individual and social rights of all people.

The struggle for human rights carries over in the Third World into the struggles of oppressed peoples for liberation, from colonialism external and internal, from poverty, from hunger, from illiteracy, from the inequalities between privileged minorities and marginally-surviving majorities.

But at the same time we must not diminish our concept of human rights by thinking of it only in terms of a struggle against structures of domination, to be explained only in terms of the need to transform a dualistic society made up of dominators and those dominated. Such an approach suggests that the disappearance of the dominators' visible power of oppression is all that is necessary for a social order to arise that is always respectful of human rights. But in fact the humanization of man, the passage from inhuman situations towards those more fraternal, is a process of constant alteration, something that is never finished, that does not have a final point of arrival.

It is not enough to perceive the dominating authority only in negative terms, as censor, obstacle, oppressor, who tells us all the things we cannot do, who forbids. The effect of this is to see only from a one-dimensional perspective, where the oppressing power is always clearly negative: a National Security state, a dictatorship, or a "strong democracy," a proletarian dictatorship whose principal role is the use of force to control its people, ordering them to accept its conditions, prohibitions, and standards.

This dominating authority is not only repressive. It also creates active or passive consensus—produces a way of seeing and expressing things that is conditioned by its structure—establishes forms of communication and relationships among the public that serve to legitimize its actions.

For this reason it is important to see what form the power networks of consensus or opposition take in a society that faces these dominating governments.

The legal system in such a society, for example, cannot be treated as a mere reflection of the social organization—it must also be recognized as part of the very form of that society. It is a complex, biased instrument that plays roles on behalf of domination as well as in defense of the dominated.

Acts of law, including agreements and declarations on human rights, must be looked at in the context of the interrelationships that surround them and all the non-legal mechanisms to which they are connected—the social realities, whether oppressive or liberating.

The international agreements concerning individual and collective human rights do establish norms and principles clearly favorable to the development of respect for the dignity of man and of all peoples. But it is important to understand the non-legal forms and mechanisms that can either favor enforcement of these agreements or serve to counteract them.

We need to find an effective methodology to link the struggle for human rights with the fight for the rights of peoples. Oppression hinders the development of human dignity. We need new insights into the structures of power and dominance that exist on many social levels so that we can discover a power that truly serves, a serving-power that will weave together the threads of social organization and expression and make them increasingly just and humane.

Our struggle must not be one only of opposition, of saying no to the dominating-power that faces us. Let us also exert a serving-power, dedicated to creating alternative means of overcoming the existing reality. In this way even the most modest may make a strong contribution to creating a society free of domination.

Such an approach might bring us to place the struggle for human rights in a historical perspective and unite it with those historical movements that can contribute to the realization of these rights.

This International Bill of Human Rights can make an important contribution not only to the struggle against human rights violations but also to the task of constructing a more fraternal and human world. It is a contribution to the struggle for the humanization of men and women in justice, freedom, and peace.

Publication of this edition of *The International Bill of Human Rights* was made possible in part by the generous support of the following individuals and organizations:

Neil Anderson

California One Foundation

Bobbie Hein

Arlan Hurwitz

Institute for Training Leaders Foundation

Martin B. Lopata and sons

Janet R. Williams

Special thanks to: Jimmy Carter, Ari Cowan, Horacio Chaves-Paz, Thomas Donilon, Tom Farer, Michael Fay, Fred Gardner, Jerry Gwathney, Barbara Hendra, Rick Hertzberg, John Klapp, Robert Lichtman, Peter Meyer, Adolfo and Leonardo Pérez Esquivel, Lori Sandstrom, Sachiko Williams.

ORDERING INFORMATION

To order additional copies of *The International Bill of Human Rights,* send $3.25 for each paperback or $9.95 for each hardcover copy, plus $1.00 total per order for shipping.

To encourage you to share *The International Bill* with others, we offer the following quantity discounts to individuals:

5 paperback copies for $15, plus $1 shipping;
10 paperback copies for $25, plus $1 shipping;
5 hardcover copies for $40, plus $1 shipping.
(If you want us to send gift copies direct to your list of names, add $1 for each separate address.)

Organizations and individuals seeking to purchase books in larger quantities should write to us for discount information.

Write to us if you'd like information on how to make a tax-deductible gift of copies of this book to school systems, libraries, churches, prisoners, human rights groups, etc.

- -

ORDER BLANK (cut out or make a facsimile)

mail to:
Entwhistle Books, Box 611, Glen Ellen, CA 95442

I'm enclosing $_____ for *The International Bill of Human Rights* as indicated below (Calif. residents add 6% sales tax):

_____ hardcover copies @ $9.95, plus $1 shipping per order

_____ paperback copies @ $3.25, plus $1 shipping per order

_____ 5 paperbacks for $15, plus $1 shipping

_____ 5 hardcovers for $40, plus $1 shipping

_____ 10 paperbacks for $25, plus $1 shipping

_____ for extra addresses @ $1 each

Name_____

Address_____

City_____ State_____ Zip_____

If you would like to be informed of future books we publish on the subject of human rights, send your name and address to:

Entwhistle Books
Box 611
Glen Ellen, CA 95442